From the Heart

An honest look at life and faith

ROB PARSONS

HODDER &
STOUGHTON

To my dearest friend, Ronnie Lockwood.
Thank you for all the years together.

First published in Great Britain in 2021 by Hodder & Stoughton
An Hachette UK company

2

A CIP catalogue record for this title is available from the British Library

Hardback ISBN 978 1 529 35815 5
eBook ISBN 978 1 529 35817 9

Typeset in Garamond MT by Hewer Text UK Ltd, Edinburgh
Printed and bound in Great Britain by Clays Ltd, Elcograf S.p.A.

Hodder & Stoughton policy is to use papers that are natural, renewable and recyclable products
and made from wood grown in sustainable forests. The logging and manufacturing processes
are expected to conform to the environmental regulations of the country of origin.

Hodder & Stoughton Ltd
Carmelite House
50 Victoria Embankment
London EC4Y 0DZ

www.hodderfaith.com

Contents

Contents

Foreword

The ancient Hebrews believed that just one organ was responsible for generating all of a person's thoughts, feelings and decisions. Everything flowed from one place in the human body, they said. Where was the hub of all this activity? Not the brain, but the heart.

'Above all else guard your heart,' King Solomon wrote, 'for *everything you do* flows from it.' (Proverbs 4:23, emphasis mine). The heart was where wisdom dwelt, where the intellectual life was centred and where your deepest feelings were processed.

Three millennia on from Solomon, our understanding of biology has grown. We now know that our inner thoughts and feelings aren't literally processed inside the organ that pumps 2,000 gallons of blood round our bodies a day. Nevertheless, our language, and way of thinking about the human heart, is still influenced by Old Testament theology. We don't speak of getting to 'the brain' of the matter, but rather 'the heart' of the matter. 'A change of heart' is far deeper than just an intellectual altering of an opinion. In the same way, when someone offers to 'share their heart', you would be right to expect a high level of candidness, openness and emotion, not just a cerebral exchanging of ideas.

In *From the Heart*, Rob Parsons draws on this biblical understanding of what the heart represents. He covers a range of subjects with wit and warmth, proving it is always more interesting to know what is in a person's heart than in a person's head. By merging insights from the scriptures with his own life experience, Rob comes across not as an 'expert', but instead a fellow traveller, a loving pastor and friend. He writes on the joy of faith and the depth of God's love for us. He warns of the dangers of cynicism and preferring competency over character. He reflects wisely on how to respond when God doesn't answer our prayers, and how to handle online criticism. Being Rob, there's plenty of stories along the way too, from the amusing – why him and Diane did all of their Christmas shopping on 1 January, to the moving – what a child rescued from the sex trade taught him about cheap grace.

Most of these fifty-five chapters were originally published as monthly columns in *Premier Christianity*. Being a magazine columnist may sound like a dream job, but as every writer knows, committing words to paper is hard. In this case, the magazine demanded something profound (but not preachy), entertaining (but not trivial) and honest (but not inappropriate). To the untrained eye, 600 words a month doesn't seem like too demanding a task, but Blaise Pascal was surely right when he said, 'I'm sorry I've written such a long letter, I didn't have time to write a short one'.

If you want to produce writing that is consistently of a high standard, that will take time, effort and editing. You will need to, like Rob, view writing as a craft, and spend hours developing the raw talents God has blessed you with. Those who want to write well must learn to scrutinise every word in their sentences, and ask themselves, 'Does this make sense? Can I say it better? Is this sentence too long? Too short?' Rob's last book (*The Heart of Communication*) was a masterclass in public speaking. Although not intended as a sequel, this book stands as an example of what outstanding Christian writing can look like.

For fifteen years, Rob Parsons blessed our readers by sharing his heart with them through his writing. I'm so pleased that this book is making those columns available to an even wider audience.

Sam Hailes
Editor of *Premier Christianity* magazine
(premierchristianity.com)

Preface

Somebody at the Gate

I have dedicated this book to a man who played a huge part in my family's life. My wife, Dianne, and I had only been married for a few years when we heard a knock on our door one night just before Christmas. When I opened it, a man was standing in the darkness. I hadn't seen him for a while, but I recognised him – he used to attend Sunday School with us when Dianne and I were children. He had learning difficulties and had spent almost all his childhood in care, but every week, our Sunday School superintendent would drive to the children's home and pick him up. To us, as youngsters, he had seemed an unusual boy, but he became a weekly presence in our young lives. His name was Ronnie.

When Ronnie was sixteen, he had to leave the children's home but was unequipped for life outside an institution. His general wellbeing deteriorated, and when he turned up on our doorstep in his late twenties he had been living in appalling conditions for some years and was now practically sleeping rough. In his right hand he clutched a black plastic bag containing all his worldly possessions, and in his left hand he held a frozen chicken. I said, 'It's Ronnie, isn't it?' He nodded. 'Where did you get your chicken, Ronnie?' He told me that somebody had given it to him for Christmas, but he had no way of cooking it. I invited him in and promised that we would cook his chicken for him. When I brought him into our living room, Dianne quickly said, 'Ronnie, why don't you stay with us tonight?' He never left.

Ronnie was to live with us for almost forty-five years. He was part of our family before our children were born and long after they became adults with children of their own. He died last year.

When he had been living with us for a little while, he got a job as a dustman. At that time, I was a lawyer and every morning I would give Ronnie a lift to work. When I got home in the evenings he would often be sitting in the same chair with a huge grin on his face. One evening I said, 'When I get home at night you're always sitting there looking happy. What amuses you so much?' He replied, 'Rob, when you take me to work in the mornings, the men I work with say to me, "Who's that who brings you to work in the fancy car?" and I reply, "Oh – that's my solicitor!'"

I have thought so much about that. I don't think Ronnie was pleased simply because he was taken to work by a lawyer. I think the reason it meant so much to him was that he'd never had a mother to take him to his first day at school or wait for him at the end of the afternoon at the school gate. When he was eleven years old he'd never had a father to ask him, 'How did it go at big school today, Son?' But now he was a man, and at last somebody was at the gate. We all need somebody at the gate.

Ronnie died in our arms. When he was born, it seemed that nobody had wanted him. Yet at the end of his life as he slipped away from us, Dianne was singing 'Yes, Jesus loves me' and we said to him time and time again, 'We love you, Ronnie'.

He was in every way a remarkable man with genuine compassion. We learnt a lot from Ronnie. Every Sunday evening without fail he helped at a homeless shelter run by our church. One particular night, he left home to go to the shelter wearing some new shoes, but when he returned home he was wearing scruffy trainers. I said, 'Where are your shoes, Ronnie?'

'I gave them to somebody who needed them,' he replied. He taught us that one day, the small and often unseen acts of kindness we do will count for far more than all the grand gestures. He taught us that in heaven's economy we don't have to have great wealth, a high IQ, or even an abundance of natural talent to affect the world around us for good. We can make a difference each day by doing simple tasks faithfully. And, of course, he taught us that our lives can be changed when we have somebody at the gate.

As well as all of that, Ronnie kept our feet on the ground. When I became a partner in the legal practice I worked for, they bought me a new car and I was dying to show it off to somebody. Ronnie sat in the passenger seat and as we drove off, I moved the steering wheel by just using my index finger. 'Do you see how easy it is, Ronnie?' I said. 'It's called Power Assisted Steering.'

'Yes, Rob, I know,' he replied. 'We have it on the dust carts.'

1

Jesus Comes for Me

I AM REVISITING ISRAEL for the first time in over twenty-five years, and as I write this I am looking over the Sea of Galilee. When I last stood here gazing across the water to the Golan Heights, I was a young lawyer and a leader in a growing church, with two small children. A quarter of a century later, the law practice is a distant memory; the toddlers, who, with a childish disregard for holy places, tossed pebbles into the water all those years ago, now have children of their own. The church that I worried about, spent hours in meetings over, and was practically brought to a nervous breakdown trying to help lead, is now growing, thriving and blessed. For some reason I have never managed to understand, heaven was not as totally dependent on me as I had imagined.

Since I was last in Capernaum and sat in the ruins of the synagogue that Jesus almost certainly preached in, two of my closest friends – men who have devoted almost all their adult lives to serving God – have fallen into affairs. Like the stones of the synagogue, the ruins of those events lie around us still.

Since I last stood on the hill where, somewhere nearby, a young teacher one day began a sermon with the words, 'Blessed are the poor in spirit . . .', I have let others down and been let down myself. I have laughed more than I would have thought possible and cried so deeply at times that I thought I would never smile again. I have made vows to God; kept some and broken some. I have sought forgiveness for sins that I've committed again within moments. I have dedicated my life to Jesus, rededicated it, and 'gone forward' at meetings more times than I can remember.

Since I last sat on the grass near where Jesus fed the 5,000 and I'd tried to imagine being one of the crowd, I have had times in my life when the living presence of Jesus faded so much that I doubted I would ever feel joy again. And I have had moments when he seemed so close that I felt I could, with Thomas, put my fingers in the marks of the nails in his hands.

Since I last visited Caesarea Philippi where, against the background of the false gods of the world, he asked,

'Whom do men say that I am?', I have had times when I was so certain of my faith that I could hardly understand how *everyone* did not believe. And I have had moments of dark doubt that threatened to suffocate my soul.

But it is none of those things that capture my mind now as I look once more across the lake. No. It is an event I have read about a thousand times before but that now blazes with fresh light for me. It occurred just before the famous incident of Peter trying to walk on the water. The disciples are in a boat on the lake at night. Jesus is not with them; he is praying in the hills above. The elements are against them, and the little boat is making slow progress in trying to reach the shore. It's not that the men aren't rowing hard – they are trying for all they are worth. But just as soon as they seem to move a little closer to the shore, a wave tosses them back.

I try to picture that scene as I gaze out over the water, and I suddenly realise that it sums up so much of my Christian life. I can almost hear myself cry out, 'It's too hard. I'm not good enough at this. I've made so little progress.' But even as I think this, the next part of the story comes to me, and I see Jesus looking up from his prayer in the hills and seeing their great predicament. Suddenly he is walking towards them; first down the hill, and then across the lake into the storm. And as he does, he is crying out, 'It is I. Don't be afraid.'

They told me in Sunday school it was vital that I come to Jesus. I'm sure they were right. But as I think back over those twenty-five years, I realise that there is something just as important . . .

It is that Jesus comes for me.

2

The Faith of My Youth

Take me back, to the place where I first received you.
. . . Take me back, dear Lord, where I first believed.

Andraé Crouch

SOME YEARS AGO, I met a wonderful Pentecostal preacher who told me that every man needed to have three men in his life: a Barnabas to encourage him; a Timothy to whom he can pass on the faith; and a Paul to mentor him. I am sure that women, too, need those three characters.

I was privileged to have some wonderful encouragers in my life and was able to help some people develop in the faith, but I didn't actually have a mentor – someone who'd look out for me, slow me down when I was going too fast, and prick the bubble of my foolish pride when

I was taking myself too seriously. I decided I needed to find a Paul.

It took me a while, but some years ago I found one. He's not much older than me, but he's a million times wiser.

When we first met, I don't think I was in very good shape. I'd become hard-hearted and a little cynical – perhaps taking holy things too much for granted. He listened to me for a while and then said, 'I'm going to pray for you the thing that Job yearned for.' My mind raced back to the oldest book in the Bible, and I hoped this wouldn't result in my having to scrape boils off my body with a bit of clay pot. I needn't have worried. Job's longing was for something very simple: 'Oh, that I knew the intimacy I had with you in the days of my youth' (Job 29:4, my paraphrase).

I remember how I'd felt in 'the days of my youth'. I'd been hungry for God and I prayed about everything – even my maths homework. I couldn't even spell the word 'cynical', and I was sure that I loved Jesus more than anybody or anything else. Since those days, a lot has happened. Some of the friends that I prayed would be healed have died. One or two of my Christian heroes have walked away from the faith. And the answers I had to difficult questions when I was sixteen seem a little less satisfactory now. It's not hard for the years to rob us of excitement, joy and wonder.

But I don't want to lose those things. I don't want knowledge to rob me of faith, experience to drain me of hope, or doubts to steal my joy. I don't want to be childish, but I *do* want to recapture, preserve and foster the kind of believing that Jesus loved so much in the young. And I certainly don't want to be gullible, but if it comes to the push, I will gladly choose that over cynicism.

It's not just attitudes that can rob my faith of freshness, but lifestyle. I remember being in a Christian leaders' retreat once when one of the speakers really challenged us. He pointed us to a verse in Ecclesiastes, 'And I saw that all toil and all achievement spring from one person's envy of another' (Ecclesiastes 4:4). We thought, 'Surely that can't be true of our little group?' We were all so busy that we could hardly stop for breath. Surely, all this activity was not being carried out just to impress somebody? Surely, it couldn't possibly be that we were somehow trying to prove ourselves?

Time and time again, I find myself considering what Jesus meant when he said to the church at Ephesus, 'You have left your first love' (Revelation 2:4, NKJV). After all, they were busy for him – they seemed to be achieving a lot. Yet, at the heart of things, something was desperately wrong. And I remember the day I realised that the words we use so often in evangelism were actually spoken to a church – this time, one in Laodicea. They were said to Christians who had somehow managed to live their lives so that Christ was left out in the cold: 'Behold, I stand at the door and knock' (Revelation 3:20, NKJV).

I don't want to live my life like that. So now, most weeks, I pray Job's 'prayer'. In the later stages of my Christian life, I find myself crying out to God . . .

'Take me back.'

3

Disappointment with God

HAVE YOU EVER thought you might stop following Jesus? I've spoken to many people who have done just that. I doubt whether any of us could really understand the complexity of experiences that contribute to that decision. And, anyway, often it won't be the result of a specific *decision*. It can come about through a slow process of which we may not even be aware.

If this experience isn't new for Christians, neither is it new for Jesus. In fact, most of those who at first decided to follow him changed their minds. John's Gospel records him turning to his twelve closest disciples and asking that poignant question: 'You don't want to leave too, do you?' (John 6:67, my paraphrase). Peter answered him, 'Lord, to whom shall we go? You have the words of eternal life' (John 6:68).

Lots of things can contribute to the experience of losing faith, but I've come to believe that often the reason is very simple: *disappointment*.

First, it may be disappointment with others. Perhaps other followers of Jesus have hurt us deeply. For many of us, the wounds we carry were not inflicted by strangers but by friends. Or it may be that someone we had looked up to and learnt from let us down badly – even turned their back on all they'd believed, trashing it in front of our eyes. And we suddenly thought, 'Perhaps it was all a lie.'

Second, I think that sometimes we lose faith because of disappointment with ourselves. We find it hard to pray, easy to sin, and feel that we let God down the whole time. Professor Lewis Smedes called this attitude 'spiritual catastrophizing'. He put it like this:

> [The 'spiritual catastrophizing'] demon speaks to me in the words of the King James Bible: 'Oh thou feckless fop of a man, surely there is no spark of spiritual strength in thee: fie on thee, fatuous wretch, for such a worm as thou there is no hope . . .' The joy-killing demon delights in making every spiritual failure fatal.*

* Rob Parsons, *The Book That Changed My Life*: '*How Can It Be All Right When Everything is All Wrong' by Lewes B. Smedes* (Authentic, 2011).

And last, sometimes people turn their back on Jesus because they are disappointed with God and feel he has let them down. I think of a man I knew who had a spiritual answer to every circumstance of life. I've never met anybody as sure of their faith, convinced that God could not only heal every disease but that he *would*. However, he had no theology of suffering. So when he walked away from the grave of his wife, he also decided to walk away from God.

I remember a telephone conversation I had with David Works. David and his wife, Mary, had four children and were about to go overseas to serve God. One Sunday morning in 2007 after their church service in Colorado Springs, they were about to drive off when they became the random victims of a young gunman. In just a few minutes, David's life changed for ever. One of his daughters was shot dead in the car, another lay dying on the ground, and he himself was so wounded he couldn't even crawl to help her.

He remembers lying on the concrete of the car park and crying out to God, 'What is going on here? We're missionaries. We're about to go around the world for you.'

He said the answer wasn't audible, but it was as clear as if it had been. He heard God say, 'David, we are not going around this. We are not going under it. And we are not going over it. We are going *through* it.'

And suddenly David had to answer a question that millions of followers of Jesus have asked themselves over the centuries: 'Can I go on following a God who allows me to go *through* things?'

David kept his faith in God. Of course, there was anger – rage even – but although there was so much that he didn't understand, for him there was no alternative. As he lay in hospital that night, he spoke to God, quoting the words of Peter we referred to above: 'I don't understand this, you're not making any sense right now. But I'm not going anywhere. *You have the words of eternal life.*'

I'm glad it was Peter who gave that reply to Jesus. I suppose you can guess why. It's because Peter is like us. One minute he's promising to die for Jesus, the next he's denying him. And one day he's curled up at the feet of the Prince of Peace and listening to the beauty of the Sermon on the Mount, the next he's slicing somebody's ear off in Gethsemane. But he went on following Jesus. He went on in spite of his disappointment with others – like the position-grabbing James and John vying for the best places in Jesus' future kingdom. He went on in spite of the disappointment with himself and that haunting memory of a courtyard, a fire and a cock crowing. And, yes, he went on even in spite of disappointment with God – when all his expectations of Jesus and his kingdom had to change so radically.

Will you or I ever stop following Jesus? Some of us will. But if I am not one of them it will be, at least in part, for a very simple reason. Even though the followers of Jesus may at times carry sharper swords than my enemies, even though, for much of my life, I feel I'm a rubbish Christian, and even though I find myself often disappointed that God doesn't answer all my prayers with a great big 'Yes', I am like Peter on at least one point: I believe that Jesus is the truth. And because of that, then for both of us it's the same: *we know there's nowhere else to go.*

4

Between You and God

IN THE MUSICAL *Blood Brothers*, the narrator looks at a group of carefree teenagers and says, 'And who'd dare tell the lambs in spring what fate the later seasons bring?' I often wished, when my children were small, that I could protect them from some of what they would have to face later in life, but I couldn't do that.

Of course, even young people's lives are not without concerns – far from it, in fact. Even in nursery school, one child is already somebody's best friend and another is rejected for the moment. Most of their artwork may comprise splodges of paint randomly daubed onto paper, but in one child's painting the outline of a cow, a horse – in fact, the beginning of a whole farmyard – can be clearly seen. Other children (and not a few parents) cast wistful eyes at the masterpiece ... and so the competition starts. Of course, this situation is not helped by parents who argue with the teacher that actually it was their child who won the egg and spoon race because the girl who came in first was holding her egg.

The truth is that the pressures of the playground follow many of us all our lives. Outwardly we may seem self-assured, but we can't shake off the gnawing feeling that, at heart, we don't match up to other people's expect-ations. When we slip into this way of thinking, our mood and enthusiasm for new tasks can be affected by what we believe others think of us. We are at the mercy of the chance comment of praise and live under the dreadful spectre of somebody's possible displeasure.

We carry out a job and we sense it has gone reason-ably well. It could be in respect of our work, church, or family life. Many people tell us they appreciated what we did, but one person says something negative – and it is that comment that we simply cannot get out of our minds. It makes us feel that we never want to write another report, preach another sermon or cook another meal for the rest of our lives.

With those thoughts taking over, we can become more concerned with what people think than with what God thinks. The Apostle Paul urged us not to make that mistake: 'Am I now trying to win the approval of human beings, or of God? . . . If I were still trying to please people, I would not be a servant of Christ' (Gal. 1:10). Just as we cannot serve both God and mammon, we cannot be effective in the kingdom unless our gaze is more often upward than over our shoulder.

Some time ago, I imagined each of my five grandchildren coming into my study at different times, not as the toddlers and babies they were then, but as adults. I pictured the conversations I'd have with them in which I'd share some of the life lessons that I've learnt – some the hard way and some that were passed on by those far wiser than me. I decided to write a book about those imaginary conversations and called it *The Wisdom House*. The last lesson of the book is about the liberation that comes with being more concerned with what God thinks than with what others think. Let me leave you with something I included there – words that are widely attributed to Mother Teresa and that used to hang on the wall in her office in Calcutta. Don't ever forget the last line.

People are often unreasonable, irrational, and self-centred. Forgive them anyway.

If you are kind, people may accuse you of selfish, ulterior motives. Be kind anyway.

If you are successful, you will win some unfaithful friends and some genuine enemies. Succeed anyway.

If you are honest and sincere, people may deceive you. Be honest and sincere anyway.

What you spend years creating, others could destroy overnight. Create anyway.

If you find serenity and happiness, some may be jealous. Be happy anyway.

The good you do today will often be forgotten. Do good anyway.

Give the best you have, and it will never be enough. Give your best anyway.

In the final analysis, it is between you and God. It was never between you and them *anyway*.

5

The Heart of a Saturday Morning

TODAY IS SATURDAY, my favourite day of the week. There, I've said it. I know that Saturday *shouldn't* be my favourite day, and I'm not really sure why this is. I think it must be something to do with that *other* day when I was growing up. The truth is that no matter how much attitudes have changed and old taboos have been banished, I still can't free myself of the nagging feeling that if I'm enjoying myself on a Sunday, I'm probably doing something I shouldn't be.

Anyway, that's not my main point at all. The main point is that not only is this my favourite day, but that I have just been doing my favourite *thing*: sitting in a coffee shop with a real newspaper, one that gets ink on your fingers, and imbibing enough Americanos to keep any normal person awake for a year. (I do understand that these admissions are getting worse. It's bad enough to have the wrong favourite day, but when one could be enjoying pleasures such as art, literature or even romance, to admit that, actually, your favourite thing is to sit by yourself once a week for forty-five minutes seems borderline deranged.)

The street on which I do my favourite thing is small, with a parade of shops on either side. For more Saturdays than I care to recall, at 9.15 a.m. I have made my way past the charity shop, the optician and the chemist towards the newsagent, at which I tarry briefly, before reaching the resting place for weary travellers that carries the rather pretentious name, Coffee#1. So why was it that on this particular Saturday morning, I began to notice people and things in such a different way?

It started with the sandwich board sign outside the pawnbrokers: 'Get cash *NOW* for your unwanted jewellery'. I gazed at the sign and wondered how many people who need cash in a hurry have *unwanted* jewellery. Was the engagement ring unwanted when it was bought in a flush of heady romance? Was the eternity ring unwanted when the young woman received it from her grandmother? Was the wedding ring unwanted when the bride first slipped it onto her husband's finger? No, they weren't unwanted then – and probably not now. The only unwanted thing relating to this jewellery is the financial pressure that causes its owner to hold it tentatively towards the pawnbroker and whisper, 'What can you give me for this?' I thought of that verse from Proverbs: 'Whoever is kind to the poor lends to the LORD' (Proverbs 19:17).

I walked on. As I neared the chemist, a man was coming towards me. He looked reasonably well dressed, but his head was down and a can was in his hand. He was holding it with his fingers wrapped around it to make it almost impossible to see its label, but as he passed me his hand moved slightly and I saw the Carling logo. It was not yet ten o'clock but the drinking had started. As I watched him go by, I thought of my friend Richard whose funeral I'd gone to not long ago. Richard was an alcoholic and I'd visited him in his dingy flat just before he died. The bottle had robbed him of almost everything he ever loved – his wife, children, home and career – but he'd looked up at me through bleary eyes and said, 'I love Jesus. You know that, don't you, Rob?'

'Yes, Richard,' I'd said. 'I know you love Jesus.'

Just outside the coffee shop, I met Angela. I hadn't seen her for many years, but we were no more than thirty seconds into our conversation before she began pouring out her heart:

We've been married for fifty-seven years but now my husband has dementia, and he's started to fall down a lot. He's in a nursing home, but the children are pressing me to have him home. I'm just not sure I can do it. Of course, they'll visit and have a cup of tea with him, but then they'll be gone.

And then she leant forward and whispered, 'The worst thing is – *the guilt*.'

My Saturday morning brought to mind an occasion at the beginning of Mark's Gospel. Jesus is staying at Peter's home. It is evening and people soon hear the news that he's in town. Soon, the little road outside the house is crowded with the blind and the lame, the dumb and the demon-possessed. They wait in their great need. And suddenly he is among them; touching them, healing them – loving them.

There is so much need in the world. People may not come to church as much as they used to, but they still need the love and touch of Jesus. As I think of that, I cannot help but imagine the centuries rolling back. We are not at Peter's house now but at the little coffee shop, and suddenly it is *him* – Jesus – coming out of it and into the street outside. And there they are – the broken, the bruised, the fearful and the hopeless – *waiting*.

6

Do You Really Believe God Loves You?

D O YOU EVER wonder what people think of you? A friend told me about a simple test by which we can find out: ask yourself what you think of *them* and it will mirror what they think of you. Do you find your friend funny, generous or loyal? Well, that's how they perceive you. Is your work colleague difficult, moody or disloyal? Well . . . you get the idea.

Of course, that test is not foolproof, but I think there may be something in it. The pastor and author A.W. Tozer suggested a similar experience with regard to God:

> What comes to our mind when we think about God is the most important thing about us . . . Were we able to extract from any man a complete answer to

the question, 'What comes into your mind when you think about God?' we might predict with certainty the spiritual future of that man.[*]

In other words, what we think about God will affect what we believe about how *he* views *us* – and that will determine the kind of relationship we have with him.

Imagine two computers. They appear identical, but before they leave the factory they have different software installed. The effect is dramatic: the minute those 'identical' computers are turned on, they behave differently. On one you can edit films, on the other you can trade shares on the world market.

Human beings are somewhat similar, except that our 'software' is written in our genes but also by teachers, friends and, perhaps most of all, parents. Some people call it our 'narrative'. And, of course, one of the strongest parts of that narrative, as Tozer suggests, is how we view God. For some of us, as soon as we wake up we hear, 'God is disappointed in you. You must spend today proving that you can please him.'

It's not hard to see why this particular narrative runs so easily in our spiritual lives; it is hardwired into every part of our human experience. We have learnt from

* A.W. Tozer, *The Knowledge of the Holy* (Bibliotech Press, 2016).

childhood that teachers praise us when we get questions right, sports coaches pick us for their teams if we are faster or stronger than our peers, and even our parents can seem to love us more when we are good.

As a child in Sunday school, I used to sing this song:

> Echo, Echo, Echo,
> Echo is my name,
> I go wherever children go,
> and always say the same.

> Echo, Echo, Echo,
> remember I am here,
> And *never* say a word,
> you don't want God to hear.

I grew up with this character called Echo. He lurked around all children, and the second we said something naughty he reported it straight to God. I knew that made God really cross. Tony Campolo, the sociologist, pastor and author, experienced something similar. He was told as a child that when you died you would come face to face with God and that God would play a video of your whole life to everybody – including your mother! My Sunday school teacher was right to tell me that God didn't want me to sin. But the really big story about God in the Bible is the fact that *he loves me*.

I believe that for many Christians, the simple truth that God loves them comes as a total surprise. Perhaps not intellectually – they know in their minds that God loves them (they can recite the verses to prove it). No, the surprise is in their hearts.

But this shouldn't be a shock to us. The Bible is the story of God's love affair with human beings. It is true that it talks a lot about sin – but that's because God hates what sin does to those he loves.

And God's love is better, bigger and more enduring than any love we have ever experienced. The steadfast love of God is mentioned 128 times in the Psalms, and Jesus warned his disciples not to think that God loved them less than human parents: 'Which of you fathers, if your son asks for a fish, will give him a snake instead? Or if he asks for an egg, will give him a scorpion?' (Luke 11:11–12). God is not in heaven to catch you out, but to love you.

I am ashamed to tell you that it has taken me almost all my adult life to begin to understand the truth that God loves me. Most mornings, I go into a quiet room and pray. I have a list of people to pray for; it's long and, to be honest, sometimes I feel as if I'm just ploughing through it. Nevertheless, when I have finished it, I have a sense of achievement – a feeling that I have, perhaps, pleased God. But God challenged me about this the other day when my grandson ran towards me. When I saw him, I was filled with joy. I swept him up into my arms and hugged him. And it was then that I felt God say to me, 'Rob, don't get too screwed up about that list. Even if you miss a few names out some days, remember that *I* know the list too. What brings me delight is to see you on your knees in prayer. I love it when you run to me like that.'

If we can understand this, it will change everything – our relationship with God and with others, and the way in which we view ourselves.

So before you go to bed tonight, ask God to gently wake you tomorrow morning with a narrative running in your brain that truly reflects how he feels about you.

He loves you.

7

You've Got Mail

'THIS EMAIL IS a violation of our community's standards.' So declared Harvard University in referring to a piece of vitriolic communication between two students. The comment resonated with me because I'd just spent time with a young man who was visibly shaken by a vitriolic email he'd had from a Christian colleague. It was largely composed of capital letters and exclamation marks.

In addition to that, I'd recently seen several other emails sent by mature Christians that were at best rude and at worst bullying. One was shown to me by a father. His face was drawn with pain as he told me about it. His son is involved in a Christian ministry that is experiencing some challenges – nothing new there. Some people don't agree with the line being taken and have said so

– nothing new, or wrong, there either. No, what was hurting this father so much was the sheer venom contained in some of the emails his son was receiving, at least one of which had accused him of an alliance with Satan.

I could hardly believe that its author, a leader I respected and admired, had penned that little bit of poison. What I'm sure of, however, is that if the writer of this letter had had to literally 'pen' it, there would have been at least several crumpled drafts in the wastepaper bin. And even then, his hand might have hovered in front of the letter box before he finally sent it on its way. But in writing the email, as soon as he'd vented his feelings he had pressed 'Send'. And within milliseconds, a small beep sounded on a fellow Christian's phone to alert him to a new email.

I recently heard a comment from a Member of Parliament who also spoke of the offensive emails he'd received from some Christians. He said, 'I don't know what kind of God those people believe in, but he is certainly not compassionate or loving.' Let me emphasise: he was not commenting on the substance of their argument, but on the way it was delivered.

I'm not whining about genuine criticism. I've been involved in leadership in the Christian world long enough to have had my fair share of critical letters. (I used to think you could almost recognise them simply by the type of handwriting or the colour of the ink!) They often followed a predictable format. First, the correspondent told you how much they appreciated you and that the only reason for writing was to uphold the good name of whatever you were both involved in. Then came a couple of paragraphs, often laced with Scripture, that basically told you that you were a heretic, a fool, or worse. Finally, the letter would wind up with something like 'Love in Christ, Basil.'

Of course, I didn't like getting those letters, but the fact is that, like it or not, there was often a grain of truth (and sometimes a lot more than a grain!) in what the writers were saying. Anyway, at least you knew they'd gone to the effort of writing the thing, sticking it in an envelope and walking to the post box. Of course, the sheer effort involved in all of those stages meant that many such a potential missive (or should that be 'missile'?) never saw the light of day. The writer either thought better of sending it or, just as likely, left it hanging around for a couple of days, then couldn't quite remember why they'd felt so screwed up and decided to watch telly instead.

Life is different now. I've just read an article by a journalist who describes watching her friends and family destroy years of relationship with a thoughtless text or

Facebook posting. As she grappled with the reasons why people would send such material, she concluded that the instant gratification of 'getting it off my chest' is so great that it often overrides considerations of perspective, kindness and even common decency. She admits: 'The truth is that I am far more likely to send a hurried email or text to a friend who has offended me than take the time to have it out with them face to face.'

We all need to be big enough and, frankly, wise enough, to take criticism, but I believe that digital technology has brought fresh dangers we are hardly aware of when it comes to giving criticism. It has to do with the sheer ease with which we can both write and post our words.

My main worry is not just for those who receive such criticism but for those of us who send it. Some religious leaders once gave Jesus a piece of their mind; in fact, they levied the same criticism at him that was sent to my friend's son 2,000 years later: they accused him of being in league with Satan himself. And it was in that context that Jesus said something absolutely terrifying: 'On the day of judgement people will give account for every careless word they speak, for by your words you will be justified, and by your words you will be condemned' (Matthew 12:36–7, ESV).

You may upset me. You may do things, write things or say things that I believe are wrong. And I may decide to let you know what I think about all of that. It may be right, or even absolutely necessary, that I do so. But if I know that what I write may hurt you, I had better be careful that nothing I say is, in Jesus' words, 'careless' – just dashed off, a piece of my mind.

When dealing with our email, we all dread the possibility of replying to all and copying someone in by mistake. We have every right to be afraid. Jesus' warning that everyone will have to give an account for every careless word is worth musing on, and I should know this: even if my computer crashes and my Sent Items folder reads 'Empty', my words will never be completely lost.

Someone has a copy.

8

A Creeping Separateness

OVER THE YEARS I have heard many people explain why they felt their marriages had come to an end. I have listened as people talked of the financial irresponsibility of a partner, the discovery of an affair, or perhaps the abuse of one kind or another that was carried out. But I have never been able to get one particular conversation out of my mind, and I think that is because of the simplicity with which the couple described the death of their relationship. The husband said, 'The strange thing is that in many ways we still love each other. It's just that over the years there has been *a creeping separateness*.'

In similar fashion, I have listened to people tell me why they no longer follow Christ. Sometimes they mentioned intellectual struggles, but they usually presented this more as a contributing factor than a driving force for their decision.

Many spoke about something I covered in chapter 3: *disappointment.* Sometimes it is disappointment with other Christians. They feel let down by the Christian community and perhaps deeply hurt by it. At times, they have equated a difficult church member with God himself. Sometimes the disappointment is with God who, it seems, has not answered their prayers: their jobs have been lost, their children have rebelled, their illnesses remain, their dreams are still unfulfilled. And sometimes the disappointment is with themselves. As one person said: 'I find it impossible to live the kind of Christian life that preachers seem to suggest is normal. I spend half my life struggling to live up to that ideal and the other half feeling guilty. I can't go on like that.'

But although those are powerful killers of faith, I believe there is a far more dangerous destroyer of relationship with God. It is best explained by that phrase: *a creeping separateness.* We begin the Christian life with such enthusiasm, but somehow, over time, our living relationship with Christ lessens. It isn't that we are not busy in Christian work – we may be insanely busy – but we know in our heart that we have lost something. It's as if we come home at night to the house of our soul, but nobody is in.

It is possible to live for many years in this condition (I've heard it described as 'running on empty') and hardly realise it. When I was once reading what Mary said outside the empty tomb – 'They have taken my Lord away . . . and I don't know where they have put him' (John 20:13) – I remember saying to myself, 'That's how I feel right now. It's as if somebody has robbed me of the Jesus I once knew, and I'm not sure how to find him again.'

An experience like that is hard, but it is possible to rediscover a relationship we may have thought gone for ever. Everything changed for Mary the second someone she thought was a stranger spoke her name, and my help, too, came from an unexpected source. One day I came across words written over two hundred years ago by the hymn writer William Cowper:

> Where is the blessedness I knew?
> When first I saw the Lord?
> Where is the soul-refreshing view
> Of Jesus and his word?

Cowper seemed to be writing about the very thing I was experiencing. It was as if he understood *a creeping separateness*. The hymn touched me deeply, and hinted at a way back. The final verses became my heartfelt prayer:

Return, O holy Dove, return,
Sweet messenger of rest;
I hate the sins that made thee mourn,
And drove thee from my breast.

The dearest idol I have known,
Whate'er that idol be,
Help me to tear it from thy throne
And worship only thee.

So shall my walk be close with God;
Calm and serene my frame;
So purer light shall mark the road
That leads me to the lamb.

9

The Wisdom of Ecclesiastes

THE *NEWS OF the World* used to have the strapline: 'All human life is here'. This statement is much better applied to the book of Ecclesiastes, which wrestles with the hope, tears and depths of humanity. Near the beginning is one of the most famous poems in the world. It starts with the two great certainties of an individual's life: 'There is a time for everything . . . a time to be born and a time to die' (Ecclesiastes 3:1–2). It ends with the two certainties of international life: 'a time for war and a time for peace' (3:8). And in an age when we are dominated by the word 'How?' – 'How can we solve this problem?', 'How can we achieve success?', 'How can I be happy?' – this ancient book asks us to consider another word: 'Why?'

But although Ecclesiastes often concerns itself with the meaning of life, it holds plenty of wisdom for the everyday issues we all have to deal with. Do you remember your mother saying to you when you were a child, 'I hear that somebody was naughty in school today?' You would reply, 'How did you know that?' And she would say, 'Oh, a little bird told me.' Wasn't that infuriating? The little bird that lived in our street didn't have time to build nests or care for its young – it spent all its time gathering information to blow the gaff on the kids it spied on. Actually, the bird never existed; it referred to an image used by the writer of Ecclesiastes: 'Do not revile the king . . . because a bird in the sky may carry your words, and a bird on the wing may report what you say' (Ecclesiastes 10:20). Catholic philosopher Blaise Pascal said, 'If all men knew what others say of them, there would not be four friends in the world.'

Ecclesiastes also has some advice about the dream that has lodged for years in the cupboard of our minds – the project we've planned to start for ages, but the time has never seemed quite right. It says, 'Whoever watches the wind will not plant; whoever looks at the clouds will not reap' (Ecclesiastes 11:4). As long as we're afraid that the wind will blow our seed away, we'll keep it safe in the decaying barn of our inner life. It's true that the seed is not exposed to risk, but its death, although slow, is as certain as if we'd stamped on it the day we first had it. In other words, the time to start sowing the seed of our idea is *never* perfect. So whether it's planting a new church, beginning a personal fitness programme or starting a business, sometimes you have to stop worrying . . . and *just do it*.

This old book understands humanity well. Which is why it says we should never ask: 'Why were the old days better than these?' It tells us simply that 'It is not wise to ask such questions' (Ecclesiastes 7:10). Many a church leader has torn out their hair as a member has whispered, 'I was here at the beginning' (apparently claiming eternal status) 'and it was so wonderful then. The worship was heavenly, yet orderly. The preaching was sound, yet compelling. And the building committee was adventurous, yet financially circumspect.' Ah, those 'old days' with their hotter summers, buses that ran on time, and young people who knew their place . . .

But why does Ecclesiastes warn us that this question is so very wrong? It is because, in yearning for an imaginary past, we are robbed of the awesome potential of changing *today*.

Ecclesiastes' wisdom about birds that carry messages, dreams, and a rosy-coloured past are all very compelling, but perhaps its most powerful phrase lies in chapter 3:11. Its strength lies in the fact that it is so simply said. It is not argued or debated. It does not invite discussion. It just explains why religion and faith will always be part of our lives as human beings.

My wife, Dianne, was fortunate enough to be in Red Square in Moscow just after the fall of the communist government in 1991 when the Russian people celebrated Christmas for the first time in seventy years. They had experienced generations of atheistic teaching and yet, at the first opportunity, crowds had gathered to sing 'Once in Royal David's City' within earshot of Lenin's tomb. It seems that it is difficult to kill the reality of God in the spirits of men and women. Why is this so? Ecclesiastes tells us the secret: we cannot help ourselves. We are utterly and finally and irrevocably made for God. There is nowhere to hide.

So what is that most powerful phrase?

'He has . . . set eternity in the human heart.'

I like this quirky little book.

10

Cheap Grace

I HAVE JUST RETURNED from Asia where I had the chance to witness the incredible work that Tearfund is doing to help care for children rescued from the sex trade. I was so moved as I met with the children, some as young as ten years old, who had been sold into sexual slavery. I also visited a ministry that works with young people who have been sexually abused within their own families or by close social contacts. It offers counsel, support and, perhaps most importantly, hope. It was, of course, both a sad and sobering experience, but all the more so because one of the counsellors said that much of this abuse was occurring within the church.

The story of one small girl touched my heart in a special way. The counsellor told me that she came from a church-going family and had been abused by her father. After years of suffering, the dreadful secret came out. She had expected that others in the church would now come to her aid, and that at last there would be an end to her ongoing trauma. The church did indeed confront her father and he admitted what he'd been doing. He asked everyone, including God, to forgive him, and said he was determined never to do it again. The church believed him – and the abuse went on.

And then the counsellor told me the comment he'd heard this small girl make: 'I'd rather have a Buddhist friend than a Christian one because they believe there are consequences to their actions.' This girl, brought up in the cradle of the church, was articulating the idea of what some have called 'cheap grace'. It is the notion that our theology of forgiveness is not robust enough and that it often leaves the victim feeling utterly let down. It's not that those who have been hurt are seeking vengeance, or that they aren't prepared to try to work through the pain of forgiving those who have hurt them. And it's certainly not that they don't realise how much God has forgiven them personally, or that they fail to acknowledge that if we do not forgive, we will not be forgiven. No, it is more that they come to believe that at both an individual and corporate level, Christians deal with forgiveness badly. It is used as a reason to handle an issue sloppily, to almost pretend it didn't happen and that everything can immediately be all right again.

I have preached forgiveness for all of my adult life. I have pleaded for it in families, in local churches, in organisations. It matters to me because I know the alternative is devastation. The old Chinese proverb is right: 'The man or woman who will not forgive must dig two graves.' And yet, as I listened to the story of a young Asian girl who was old before her time, I was challenged as to how often we have made it sound too easy, too instant – too cheap.

I think now of a woman who said this to me:

I am trying to forgive my husband for leaving me for another woman, but what I find so hard is that other Christians just seem to have shrugged their shoulders. He and the new woman in his life are totally accepted, and in some ways I believe that's right. Yet, it's just that 'forgiveness' seems to have turned out to be everybody acting as if nothing has really happened. But he has broken my and our children's hearts.

I know there are no easy answers to these issues. All I am saying is that, having talked about forgiveness for so many years, I was suddenly faced with a young girl on the other side of the world who caused me to rock back on my heels and who said, in essence, 'Don't give your forgiveness so cheaply that you join in my abuse.'

And I can't get her out of my mind.

11

Bag for Life

IT WAS THE kind of Sunday morning meeting where anybody (well, anybody *male*) could stand and give 'a short word'. I was eighteen years old.

I had never even thought of taking part in the service before, but now I felt a compulsion to say something. It was hard to gauge when to stand up; get it wrong and you could end up speaking at exactly the same time as somebody else. I waited for a gap and stood, shaking, to deliver what I felt God would have me say: a little encouragement from Luke's Gospel. When I sat down I felt relieved it was over and also excited that God might have used me. But I had no idea what was about to happen next.

Unfortunately, I had not quite understood the dress code for this particular meeting. Instead of a collar and tie, I was wearing a red polo-neck sweater. This fact came home to me when an older man immediately leapt to his feet and began talking about an incident in the life of Joseph. The story records that when commanded to see the King of Egypt, Joseph had 'shaved and changed his clothes'.

I'll be honest with you, it went completely over my head at first – until the speaker turned, glared at me, and said that when we go to see the King, it's important to dress properly.

What he did in that moment was to take something from the rucksack on his back that was marked 'Proper Christianity' and load it onto me. But he's not the only one carrying baggage. I have a bag too – and so do you. The bag contains, among other things, the way I have been taught to worship, to tithe, my attitude to alcohol, the way I use my money, the films I watch, the way I believe we hear God's voice, and the way I approach politics.

In my more foolish moments, I kid myself that I have managed to lose the bag – that I am now free of it. But the truth is that the old bag will not so easily be laid down. Each of us is tied more closely to our culture than we can possibly imagine.

The great danger – both to me and others – is when I decide to hang my bag on the shoulders of another Christian. Jesus caught the religious leaders of his time doing this and he hated it: 'You load people down with burdens they can hardly carry' (Luke 11:46). The dreadful implication was that God looked at things differently to them and that maybe the bags they carried were filled with all the wrong stuff anyway.

As I write this, I am in Hong Kong airport, about to fly to New Zealand and Australia to present the message I wrote about in my book *Bringing Home the Prodigals*. I have already been to other countries around the world this year speaking on the same theme. Everywhere I go, I meet prodigals who had tried hard to carry the 'Proper Christianity' bag that others put on their backs, but eventually the bag had become too heavy and they had laid it down. Because they had done this, they believed they had disappointed God, so they left the church. When they tell me their story, I ask them what was in the bag they'd carried. What was it that people had told them mattered to God? Sometimes their answers make me cry.

It seems to me that one of our most urgent prayers should be, 'Lord, help me to truly know what matters to you and, if necessary, lay down my life for it. But help me also to recognise what is just my particular bag.'

Dr R.T. Kendall summed it up for me. He told me that when some German Christians saw a group of American Christians with all their gold and jewellery on, they were so shocked they dropped their cigars in their beer.

12

The Greatest Gift of a Parent

'WHAT IS THE greatest gift a parent can give a child?' That was the question I asked at one of Care for the Family's parenting events. The most common reply by a long way was 'love'.

I'm sure it's the right answer, but I'm convinced there is also another great gift: *acceptance*. If children don't feel accepted by their parents, it is almost impossible for them to feel loved by them. One of the greatest services we can do for our children is to send them into adulthood believing that at least we, their parents, accept them for who they are.

I heard recently about one mum who'd had quite an evening with her fifteen-year-old son. 'We'd spent the best part of an hour arguing about his outrageous hair and dreadful clothes,' she said. 'We simmered in silence for ages, then both collapsed laughing after he yelled, "Mum, I just want to be different like everybody else!"'

We all crave to be accepted and somebody has convinced us that what we look like and what we achieve are the things that make us acceptable.

I Accept the Way You Look

One of the greatest pressures on children in modern society is the way they look. These days it's not enough to be a great footballer; you have to be a great, *good-looking* footballer. And it's not just football. From her infancy, your daughter will assess from a million messages – some screamed at her from adverts, some whispered in school playgrounds and most unsaid – whether or not she is 'beautiful'. Unless that child is destined to be one of the few who meet the standard, she'll have to do battle with the world if she is to hold on to her self-esteem. She ought not to have to do battle in the home.

How do we decide whether we are acceptable and have worth? The answer is that we perceive this from outside ourselves – from others – especially from those we love and respect. And what makes life particularly hard for our children is that so often when their self-esteem is at its most vulnerable, their peers are at their most hurtful.

I doubt we'll ever be able to do much to change the cruelty of the very young, but life should be different around our parents. I am saddened when I hear parents make derogatory comments, even in a humorous vein, about the physical appearance of their children – especially in front of others.

I remember Dianne complimenting a teenager on her new outfit. The girl smiled but her mother poked a finger at her tummy and said, 'It'll look even better when she does something about that.' Of course, a parent will want to help a child who is seriously overweight or who has a bad attack of acne, but somehow we have to let our children know that we love them anyway. That involves us being manifestly proud of them when they are at their gawkiest, most awkward, and especially if their particular features don't happen to fit with what society, at present, calls attractive.

I Accept You Irrespective of What You Achieve

The second way that we show our children whether or not they are accepted is by our attitude to their achievements. So one of the most testing aspects of parenthood is to balance motivating our offspring to reach their potential without instilling in them the belief that our love for them is conditional on how they perform.

Many children do need motivating in the area of school work and it's often difficult to manage this. It's possible to be too easy-going and not push a child hard enough, or to push too hard and pressurise them. But in the middle of all the yelling, the blackmail, and the forced study-guides for breakfast – our children should know for a certainty that they are loved *anyway*.

Of course, it's good to give children opportunities, and activities like piano lessons and football coaching can be wonderful, so long as we don't make it hard to just have fun. The main aim should be that our children enjoy playing the piano and being on the football field, not that they end up at the Festival Hall or playing at Wembley.

Acceptance doesn't mean that we don't try to encourage our children to get better grades, or motivate them to achieve their best. It doesn't even mean that we don't hope they will change in some ways. But it does mean that we do not put on them the burden of being someone they cannot be.

We send our children into a world that will continually judge them. They will be forced to ask themselves, 'Am I clever/determined/successful/sociable enough?' And, of course, 'Am I attractive enough?' Matching up to the demands of others is a wearisome business. But we do our children a wonderful service if we send them into that world with an unshakeable belief that there is at least one person who, irrespective of their grades, weight or athletic genius, loves and accepts them unconditionally. It really is the greatest gift. Most of us, as adults, are still searching for somebody to love us like that.

13

Study Talks

M Y SON LLOYD is now an adult with children of his own, but when he was a child we would sometimes have what he came to call 'study talks'. On these occasions I would say, 'Lloyd, can we have a word? Come into the study for a moment.' He told me one day he hated hearing those words – they were often a precursor to a mini-lecture on homework, smoking, cheeking his mother, or, perhaps even worse, his old man trying to get him to take a longer view of life beyond the party he was going to that evening. And yet, as I said to him one day, 'There's something worse than study talks and that is having a father who doesn't much care what you do.' I remember a girl of fifteen who was sleeping rough on the streets of London saying, 'My parents wanted me in at ten o'clock and I

[50]

hated that, but I wish somebody cared what time I came in now.'

God gives me study talks. There are times in my life when he feels the need to let me know that I've crossed a line. Sometimes he uses other people or a passage of Scripture to let me know what he feels. On other occasions, it's a thought direct to my heart that rocks my complacency. But often it is the ordinary circumstances of life that he uses to get my attention. I wouldn't blame you if you said, 'Well, these are just coincidences – they could happen to anybody.' Perhaps you're right, but in my life at those times I've had no doubt that God is doing what every parent dares not dodge: he is exercising a little discipline.

I normally seem to hear from him like this when I behave in certain ways. One example would be where I simply take him for granted. In my heart I say, 'He loves me so much, he forgives so easily, I can probably go on doing this . . .' The Bible warns against 'testing God' – seeing how much you can get away with. The problem with this seems to be that, for a while, the love and forgiveness thing seems to be working perfectly well and then suddenly it's as if you push God one step too far.

Another example would be if I get cynical. Cynicism is corrosive. There are times in my life when I've been gullible and times when I've been cynical. I believe the latter is far worse. I was at a friend's house for Sunday lunch the other day and before we ate he sighed wearily and said, 'Well, I suppose we'd better say grace.' I think I almost heard heaven say, 'Keep it.' I wondered if he'd ever been invited into God's study.

But by far the most common, and the most painful, example of occasions when God lets me know that I've crossed a line is when I get proud. In fairness, this is something I've been warned about well in advance; as a child, I was told that 'God hates the proud' and 'God despises a haughty spirit'. The problem with pride is that when it happens it's hard to spot it in yourself because you are so caught up in your own greatness. It's only when God brings me down to earth and makes me realise that I am totally dependent on him that I feel like kicking my own backside.

I pray a little prayer these days: 'Lord, your discipline hurts; make me a faster learner.'

Of course, we need wisdom here. Generally, the bad things that happen in life are just that – bad things that happen – and we'll drive ourselves crazy if we interpret every unpleasant event as God trying to get our attention. But the truth is that sometimes he *does* discipline us. The Bible says, 'He does it because he loves you, so don't despise it' (Hebrews 12:5–6, my paraphrase).

Max Lucado puts it like this, 'It is true that God loves us as we are, but he loves us too much to leave us as we are.'*

The good news is that God is my father. The bad news is that he seems to be taking the job seriously.

* Max Lucado, *Just Like Jesus* (Thomas Nelson, 2003).

14

Nasty Christians

W HY ARE WE Christians often so nasty to each other? Imagine there is some friction in our local church. Typically, it will be regarding the style of leadership, the music, the new building project or the youth work. But whatever it's about, the issue is often not the major problem – wherever there are groups of people there will always be differences of opinion. No, the real problem is that, time and time again, people who have spent years talking about grace, reading books on grace, and going to conferences on grace are suddenly faced with situations where they need to be gracious, but instead they become . . . nasty. Followers of the Prince of Peace suddenly decide to go to war. They gather a little army around them, have war councils in their living rooms, and plan the downfall of those they oppose, all the while praying for 'wisdom, guidance and, above all, that Your name, Lord, may be honoured'.

A great place to see some of this played out is in church AGMs. Some have the flavour of cup-ties. It's true that the opposing teams do not actually wear different colours, but they do sit together in 'the stadium' and predictably roar their approval or boo according to how their team is doing. I have contrasting memories of such occasions. I recall the times when godly men and women expressed deeply felt beliefs, but did so with that fruit of the Spirit: *kindness*. Their remarks might have been direct – tough even – but they were gracious. I also remember occasions when people behaved so badly and spoke with such venom that if the local church were a school it would have excluded them.

I was quite young when I first saw Christians treating each other in this way, and I remember thinking how passionately they must believe in what they were arguing for. In later life, though, it dawned on me that often the issue doesn't have anything to do with the item on the agenda at all. Those who complain that the worship is too exuberant, and eventually leave, often end up joining the church down the road that worships while swinging from the chandeliers! No, the real issue is much deeper – it is about relationships. Some people are simply not prepared to strive to understand, build bridges with, and show care and concern to those with whom they disagree.

Church is not meant to be that way. Jesus talked about inviting all sorts of people to your parties – not just your friends. Like-minded people having fun together can be found in any old club, but life in God's kingdom is meant to be different. This kingdom is about letting enemies join in, going the extra mile, and what, in *The Message* edition of James chapter 4, is called the 'Royal Rule' – love others as you love yourself. What it is not about is a group of people with similar views feeding each other's discontent. Paul expresses this powerfully: 'I have a serious concern to bring up with you, my friends, using the authority of Jesus, our Master. I'll put it as urgently as I can: you *must* get along with each other. You must learn to be considerate of one another, cultivating a life in common' (1 Corinthians 1:10, *The Message*). We need to treat this seriously. We are all capable of behaving badly, but it is not something to be swept under the carpet or excused with 'Oh, that's just Jack – he really cares for this place at heart.'

This matters to God. It's why James says, 'Don't bad-mouth each other, friends. It's God's Word, his Message, his Royal Rule, that takes a beating in that kind of talk. You're supposed to be honouring the Message, not writing graffiti all over it' (James 4:11, *The Message*).

It's not hard to work out why these early church leaders attached such importance to this teaching. Even if they were not present themselves, they had heard what happened at Jesus' last Passover meal. They knew that he, the Lord of Glory, had washed the disciples' feet and then said, 'Now that I, your Lord and Teacher, have washed your feet, you also should wash one another's feet . . . As I have loved you, so you must love one another' (John 13:14 and 34). Within twenty-four hours Jesus was dead. This message had mattered so much to him that he'd told it to them *then*.

We sometimes excuse others and ourselves in this area by saying, 'It's important to stand up for what we believe is true.' Yes, it is. But it can't be right to stand up for one bit of truth while simultaneously trashing another.

15

The Non-poetic Will of God

EARLY THIS MORNING, and for no apparent reason, a character from my past came to mind, a Welsh evangelist called David Shepherd (not to be confused with the former Bishop of Liverpool and England cricketer). He is long-since dead but, even now, I can hear his sonorous voice booming out across the chapel, and I can picture the twinkle in his eye that you could see from the pews at the back.

I first encountered David when I was nineteen and playing rhythm guitar in a Christian band called The Proclaimers (we should have sued the later band that stole our name!). We were about to perform at a small church where David was preaching, and the five of us were squashed in the vestry with him and the pastor before the meeting began. When we started praying,

David suddenly got on his knees and the rest of us immediately followed suit. It was then that I heard strange, muffled sounds coming from him. At that time, charismatic renewal was crossing the nation and I hadn't witnessed any examples of charismatic expression in the little Brethren assembly I attended, though I had heard plenty of stories about it. When we'd finished praying, I whispered to him, 'Reverend Shepherd, were you praying in tongues?' He roared with laughter. 'No, son – that was *Welsh*!'

He could be very direct indeed. The story is told of his being in the village grocer's shop and hearing the shopkeeper say to a customer, 'What terrible weather we're having. We deserve better than this.' David had boomed across the counter, 'Mrs Harries, if the good Lord gives you what you deserve, I'll be burying you on Tuesday.'

I spent quite a bit of time with him over the years and was fortunate to be at a service in a tiny chapel when he gave one of the few sermons in my life that I can actually remember (including those I've preached myself!). He was speaking about what he called 'The non-poetic will of God'. He said:

Fairy stories end with 'And they all lived happily ever after', but God's will is not always like that.

Someone may believe they are called by God to go as a missionary to Africa, but after six months they become ill and have to come home. People say, 'It obviously wasn't God's will.' But how do you know that? Maybe it *was* God's will – and in that short time, lives were touched that only He knows about.

And then David said something I have never been able to get out of my mind, 'You can't assess whether you are in the will of God by whether things turn out well or badly.' He was right. If, on Good Friday, you had taken a snapshot of Jesus' life – a life 100 per cent in the will of God – you could be forgiven for believing he had got it wrong.

David's words have comforted me and others when faced with a situation that has not turned out as we'd hoped. Maybe we had got it wrong – but not *necessarily*.

But in the good times of life when God's blessing has seemed to pour out on my endeavours, David's words have also caused me to ponder a different message: if it's true that we are not necessarily *out* of God's will when things turn out badly, we cannot therefore assume we are *in* his will when things go well. Apparent success is not a safe measure of obedience to God.

Let me bring a smile to your face with one final story I have of David Shepherd. He wasn't a fan of what he called 'new-fangled' translations of the Bible, and I remember hearing him preach from John 14. David said, 'Jesus told the disciples, "In my Father's house are many mansions."' And then, half-smiling and half-scowling as he looked at us sitting in the pews, he added, 'Not "rooms", mark you, "*mansions*"!'

16

'Why, My Soul, Are You Downcast?'

WHEN SHE WOKE on that Sunday morning, Susan lay in bed for a while and wondered why she felt as she did. Normally she'd spend a few moments praying, but today it was just too hard.

Three hours later, walking into church with her two children, she realised they were late again, but she was past caring and all but fell into a seat in the back row. For some reason, getting the kids to school and herself to work by 9 a.m. on a weekday was done with military precision, but to get to church by 11 a.m. on a Sunday seemed all but impossible and always ended up with her yelling, screaming – and then feeling guilty.

Practically comatose in her chair, she suddenly realised that she was the only one sitting. The rest of the congregation were on their feet, some with hands raised upwards, singing a song about winning battles. She struggled through two verses and then it hit her – a feeling deep in her being of utter loneliness and isolation, from everyone around her and especially from God. She said under her breath, 'I just don't feel part of all this' and for a moment she had an overwhelming desire to grab the children and just leave.

I wonder whether what she felt that day were echoes of the emotions experienced by the poet who wrote, 'Why, my soul, are you downcast? Why so disturbed within me?' (Psalm 42:5). It seems to me that the psalmist was saying something like this: 'I really don't know why I feel as I do, but something is wrong in my very being. If you ask me to explain what it is, I won't be able to. I feel a mixture of sadness and fear, and I'm just not sure why.'

I sometimes feel this way myself and the strange thing is that when it happens it's hard to put my finger on the cause. As with Susan, such periods are often connected with something of a breakdown in communication between myself and God, and that's so difficult because it's at that very time when I need him most. It's as if somebody has pulled up the drawbridge and, though I'd love to get into the castle, I'm left standing outside.

So, my soul, why *are* you downcast? Have I done some great wrong that is now haunting me? Well, of course, that could be so. Or is it that I am a spiritual cissy and I really need a kick in the backside and to be told to just get on with it? (If you think it will work, kick me now!) Or is it that I'm just plain tired?

As I look back, I can see that life *has* often been incredibly busy. I may have been responding to the needs of others, perhaps I've been hurt a little along the way or experienced special pressures, but whatever has happened seems to have taken the wind out of my sails. One minute I'd been scudding along on a smooth sea under a clear blue sky, and now suddenly the breeze has stopped. I'm drifting and I've lost direction.

If I stay busy, I feel reasonably all right. The sheer activity helps in so many ways: it stops me thinking, it gives me a sense that I'm achieving something and that life is basically still on course. But when the busyness stops, when I come home to myself, when I lie in bed in the early morning darkness, the old fears and the old sadnesses come to haunt me.

The psalm begins with such a powerful image. It is of a thirsty, exhausted deer, its tongue out, panting and hoping against hope that around the next hill there will be a valley with streams of water. The mystery is that at the very time when, in so many ways, we feel distant from God – we feel the need of him more than ever.

Well, Lord, here I am – outside the castle when the party is going on inside, stranded in the middle of the sea with limp sails at the mercy of every current, and thirsty – desperately thirsty – for you.

The final verse says, 'Put your hope in God, for I will yet praise him, my Saviour and my God' (v. 11). It is almost as if the psalmist is saying, 'Don't give up – you *will* come through this.'

Perhaps, like me, you are grateful to the poet who wrote those words so long ago, sharing his heart in a way that touches our lives today. Suddenly, we understand this is not just *our* experience; others have been there and come through it. And the very second we realise this, our head lifts a little for, although we are still dry and thirsty, somehow we can smell water on the wind. Even though we are feeling adrift, we can imagine again sails full of wind, power and direction. And although we are still standing alone, out of the silence we can hear the faint sounds of a drawbridge being lifted.

17

Congratulations!

A FRIEND OF MINE told me a fascinating story. He'd been preaching at a church one Sunday and was standing at the back, shaking hands with people as they left. He watched as one woman approached him, obviously with something on her mind. She paused and then said, 'I believe God has given me a word for you.'

Over the years, he has had quite a few people say this to him and he got ready to hear a rebuke or warning. Lyndon smiled at her. 'Please share it with me.'

'Well,' the woman said. 'God wants to say one word to you: "*Congratulations!*"'

Lyndon was totally taken aback. It was the last thing he'd expected to hear, not because he believed he'd never done anything that could possibly please God, but because he didn't expect God to tell him so.

Why was my friend so surprised? I believe it was because, like many of us since becoming Christians, we have acquired a lopsided view of the way God deals with us. We have been taught to recognise when God is *dis*pleased with us: when he is disappointed, grieved or just plain angry. In other words, we have been urged to recognise our *sin*. But although it's true that we do need to be sensitive to the things we do wrong, recognising our sin is not enough to make us holy. For that, we must also learn to discern when we please God – when we do things that bring him satisfaction.

This is not only a theological truth. One of the best-selling business books written is a slim volume that can be read in half an hour, *The One Minute Manager*. In it, the authors, Ken Blanchard and Spencer Johnson, propounded their belief that in the world of business most managers operate by catching people doing something wrong and criticising them for it. But they suggest that the better and most effective way to get the best out of people is to catch them doing something right and praise them for it. They talk about the effectiveness in work situations of taking just sixty seconds a day to tell people when they are doing well: 'That report was spot on. Thanks.' 'Great talk today!' Yet so many of us find it hard to praise – a friend, a church leader, even a husband or wife.

[67]

That same piece of advice, 'Catch them doing something *right*', was also given to Dianne and me years ago by a parenting expert with regard to building a strong relationship with our children and giving them confidence. He was particularly talking about the more testing child who is generally only used to negative comments: 'Don't hit your sister!', 'Don't gobble your food!', 'Don't speak to me like that!' The problem with this is that when the ear never hears praise, the heart loses the will to try.

Years ago, I went with a guide into the Sinai desert. It was a fascinating journey, and I vividly remember one experience in particular. The guide stopped the jeep and showed me a special bush. He told me that this plant had a rare ability, one which ensured its survival in that hostile environment. Quite simply, it had learnt to live with very little water. When a drought came, other vegetation would quickly wither, but this bush died in sections; perhaps half of it would close down and the rest would use whatever moisture it could find. And then, as the drought progressed, the plant would shut down other parts of itself until finally there might be just a single stem alive, waiting for the rain. When the rain came, the seed pods on that stem would explode and send new life bursting into the desert again.

I often meet people who are like that plant. But instead of water, what they crave is a little appreciation.

They long to hear an affirming word of encouragement, and if or when it is spoken, it can change not just their day but their life. The book of Proverbs talks about kind and encouraging words having the power to bring 'healing to the bones' (Proverbs 16:24). A simple word of encouragement can penetrate to the very heart of our being.

Most of us know that. We understand that what we say to people affects them. So why do so many of us find it hard to give a simple word of encouragement to others? To catch people doing something – however small – *right*? Perhaps we're uncomfortable about giving praise, feeling that it's all a bit too emotional. Perhaps nobody has ever praised *us*, so we find it hard to affirm someone else. (Maybe we are scared they will ask for a pay-rise!) Or perhaps we enjoy far more the satisfaction of pointing out the error, the poor choice of clothes, the wayward child's behaviour, the slight mistake in Sunday's sermon. In bringing others down, we somehow feel lifted ourselves.

Yet, even if sometimes we are a bit like that, we all have within us the power to change. We can lay aside our sarcasm (which, for too long we have called 'wit'), our 'helpful' comments 'because I simply want the best for you', and even our incessant 'I think God might want me to tell you this . . .' Instead, we can discover the sheer joy of bringing words of life to somebody who is dry and thirsty.

I wonder if there might be somebody we know – a friend, a child, a husband, a wife, a church leader or a work colleague – who feels like that plant in the desert. Perhaps we can help. If so, it won't be just the sound of our footsteps coming towards them that they'll hear. It will be the life-changing, soul-refreshing, bone-healing sound of . . . *rain*.

At his baptism, Jesus heard the most wonderful words: 'This is my Son, whom I love; with him I am *well pleased*' (Matthew 3:17). I know God was speaking of his sinless-ness, but I can't help but believe that he wants each of us to know whenever he is pleased with us.

I have spent much of my Christian life believing that God is probably not very happy with me – and on many occasions, I'm sure he hasn't been. But as I get older, I sometimes catch myself praying:

Lord, if ever you see me doing anything that pleases you, even if I'm doing it by accident, help me to be so attuned to you that somehow I feel your pleas-ure. I know you will let me know when I do wrong, but if ever I bring you satisfaction then, by your grace, help me to recognise that as well – and sense your smile.

18

Worry Wars

THERE ARE FOUR basic emotions: anger, fear, happiness and sadness. I wonder which of them affects us most. I think that for many of us it is fear. The strange thing is that so often it's hard to put our finger on what we are actually afraid of; it's simply that somewhere deep inside us there is an ever-present gnawing anxiety. I remember my children reading the *Mr Men* series of books. One of the characters was called Mr Worry. This dear man was plagued by fear. He would worry about his car, his dog, his house, his dinner. And when he had nothing to worry about, he got even more concerned, for he was sure he had forgotten something important and that bothered him more than anything.

I sympathise with Mr Worry. Sometimes when I am lying in bed in the morning, I imagine having a conversation with someone. They say something that annoys me, and I reply angrily. They shoot back a stunning comment, and I deliver a withering riposte. Suddenly those thoughts will run away with me and I start to worry about it all. Then, just as a headache is beginning to form over my right eye, I realise that the whole thing has only occurred in my mind. Nobody has said anything nasty to me at all. I have not *actually* had a row with anybody. In fact, there is no real problem, and it's probably time to get out of bed.

I've had those runaway thoughts hundreds of times. I've had them before annual church meetings, when I imagine battles between opposing camps. (The actual events often turned out to be far less entertaining.) And I've had runaway thoughts about my health. In fact, when I was a child we had something in our home called *The Doctors' Book* in which you could look up the symptoms of various ailments. Every time I consulted the thing, I became convinced that I had not only the illness I was searching for, but the one on the facing page as well.

And I've had runaway thoughts when my children were teenagers and were a little late coming in at night. About ten minutes after Lloyd's curfew I would smile nervously at Dianne and start to make some tea, saying, 'He'll be in soon.' And then, just as I was filling up the kettle, my thoughts would race off and within moments

I would imagine police cars pulling up at my door, hospitals ringing me with news of accidents, or phone calls from Gretna Green saying, 'We've tied the knot. Do you want to chip in some money for the honeymoon?'

Jesus said a fascinating thing about fear: 'Do not worry about tomorrow, for tomorrow will worry about itself. Each day has enough trouble of its own' (Matthew 6:34). He was being practical and saying in essence, 'Don't worry about tomorrow because you have enough to worry about *today*.' So many of our runaway thoughts – our fears about future events – may never materialise. But we've often spent so long worrying about them, they have drained us. Mark Twain said, 'Most of my tragedies have never happened to me.'

When the early explorers drew their maps, they would draw a boundary line at the furthest point they'd reached and write: 'Beyond this there may be dragons.' They had never seen a dragon, and they had never discovered a dragon in the new places they'd explored thus far, but now they had reached uncharted regions – and the future was unknown. When they eventually got to those new territories, they were often places of wonderful beauty, rich resources and staggering opportunity. But until then, these undiscovered lands were represented by those six words on the edge of the map: 'Beyond this there may be dragons.'

The Bible tells us not to live our lives like this – allowing fear to take over. It says, 'take captive every thought to make it obedient to Christ' (2 Corinthians 10:5). I wonder if part of that could involve catching those thoughts *before* they run away with us.

19

The Day I Met a Wise Teenage Mother

SOMETIMES GOD AMBUSHES us. It happened to me in Zambia. It didn't surprise me that I felt emotional; I find I cry more easily as a man than I ever did as a child. And it wasn't exactly the poverty that shocked me, although the Tearfund colleague I was travelling with told me I had seen some of the poorest people on the face of the earth. My ambush came from a child who taught me the heart of what it means to be a parent.

Stacey had lost her father to AIDS eight years previously. He was in the military and when he died some officials had called to collect things he'd had that belonged to the army. Apparently, his family didn't matter. 'But they didn't want us – my mother and the six children,' Stacey commented. Three years ago, Stacey's mother had died. Her relatives wanted to share the children around, but the kids wouldn't hear of it. They said they must stay together.

Stacey takes care of the two girls, and her sister Dwalgu has responsibility for the boys.

I went into a tiny room and saw a clothes horse with washed underwear on it – all very worn and all spotlessly clean. On a nearby shelf was a jar with six toothbrushes in it. I could have seen that sight in many homes in the United Kingdom, but it was as if normality had to fight and kick in order to have a place among this poverty and constant threat of death. These two young women were trying to give their brothers and sisters more than survival – they were striving to give them a home.

I asked Stacey what was the most difficult thing about her situation. 'Oh,' she said, 'the girls want clothes and the boys want money.' I have heard that complaint from hundreds of parents but never before when clothes could mean two odd shoes for school and money that was obtained by selling a little paraffin outside the house in an effort to make 10p a day.

As Stacey spoke with us, her younger sister Angela, aged fifteen, lay against her, with Stacey's arm around her. They were both beautiful, and yet so very vulnerable. I asked Stacey whether she ever spoilt the youngest boy, aged ten. Stacey replied with all the seriousness of one who has learnt big lessons fast. She said, 'No – he has to make his own way in life. He works hard at school. He is number one in his class.' We talked about the loneliness of having to be a parent at such a young age, without other adult help. She said, 'I miss my mother and my father; but we can do it. We cannot live in the past – we have to look forward.'

Another member of the team asked her if she ever thought of marriage. 'Yes,' she said, 'but whoever takes me must take my brothers and sisters. I know this will require a special man, but that is what I am praying for. I want a husband, not just a relationship.'

I sat and listened to her as though I was at the feet of an old woman sharing her years of wisdom. The moment was too precious to miss. I said, 'Stacey, in the United Kingdom I run seminars for parents – thousands of people come to them. If you could pass on to them any piece of advice, what would it be?' Stacey smiled and spoke without hesitation as if she had known the answer all of her life:

You must be there for your children. If you are not there for them, any advice you give doesn't work. There must be love – that way you will feel what your children are feeling. If you give your children to a maid and you leave them with her, she may care for them, but they miss out on love.

And so I, who had spent much of my life talking and writing about parenting, who came to Africa to help children, was ambushed by a young girl who was a mother too young, but who had somehow captured the heart of parenthood in a way that we in the West often never fully grasp. I suddenly felt poor.

'Stacey,' I said, 'I will tell parents about you for the rest of my life.'

She smiled.

20

A Simple Man

I REMEMBER HEARING BILLY Graham tell of an incident that happened while he was in a city for one of his crusades. He was in the lift of a large hotel together with a colleague and some strangers, presumably hotel guests. As the lift reached the ground floor, one of the guests said, 'I hear that Billy Graham is staying in this hotel.'

Billy smiled and said, 'I'm Billy Graham.'

There was a pause as the man looked Billy up and down, but finally he replied, 'Oh – I expected more.'

Billy told the story as an amusing incident, but for some reason the man's comment to him that day has stayed in my mind. It really hit me again the day after Billy Graham died. John Humphrys was conducting an interview on the *Today* programme on Radio 4 and related an occasion when he had gone to listen to Billy Graham at Earl's Court. As he described the impression the evangelist had had on him, he used the same words as the man in the lift: 'I expected more.'

Those two men were not the only ones to have felt that way. Time and again, I have heard people ask the question, 'Why does God use him so powerfully? He's not the greatest preacher I've ever heard.' Billy Graham himself would agree. He said, 'I am not a great preacher, and I don't claim to be a great preacher. I'm just communicating the gospel in the best way I know how.'

I honestly don't think Billy Graham cared very much what people thought of him. The only sense in which it did matter to him was in respect of whether his life might reflect badly in some way on the one he served. And if it is true that he didn't care very much about others' opinion of him, then it would explain, at least in part, the incredible freedom he had in dealing with people – whether it was the press, presidents or those he came across in his everyday life. He looked to me like a man at ease with himself.

On the day that Billy died, Dr R.T. Kendall told me that one of the highlights of his ministry was when Billy came to preach at his church.

He spent an hour and forty-five minutes alone with me in my vestry. When I went home, my wife,

Louise, asked, 'What was it like to meet Billy Graham?' I took a few seconds to ponder her question before I replied. 'He's so simple. *He is so simple.*' By that I mean uncomplicated. Unpretentious. He signed my Bible that day, adding Philippians 1:6 to his name: 'being confident of this, that he who began a good work in you will carry it on to completion until the day of Christ Jesus'. Then he prayed for me.

What was the secret of Billy Graham's life? Perhaps R.T. Kendall has given us a clue in that word 'uncomplicated'. Billy loved God more than anybody or anything else, and this meant that, in the very best way, as far as he was concerned, you could take him or leave him. In other words, he was more concerned with what God thought than he was about the thoughts of the man in the lift. Sometimes I ache for that freedom.

I understand that he had asked for just a single word to be written on his gravestone to describe his life: 'Preacher'. I think he could equally have chosen four words:

'Just as I am.'

21

Kick the Leaves

I T WAS A time in my life where I felt low, stressed and had little peace. One day a friend said to me, 'You live such a busy life – you seem to have lost the ability to even spend time with *yourself*.' He suggested that I took a little time each day to 'kick the leaves'. He said, 'Maybe take a walk in a park. Don't try to think of some new strategy for the next year, or jot down ideas for a new book. Just amble.'

It seemed a luxurious, even a wasteful, image that my friend painted that day, but I became convinced that he was right. I'm sure that the reason many of us find it hard to pray – to spend time alone with God – is that we find it difficult to be alone with *ourselves*. Activity and busyness enter every area of our lives; we cannot simply be still.

Modern gadgets feed our addiction. The other day at church I watched as a friend sitting next to me emailed, Googled, Facebooked, WhatsApped, and I don't know what else, as the speaker expounded the book of Isaiah. Of course, to most eyes he appeared to be using his smartphone to follow the text on his Bible app, jotting down helpful reflections or tweeting particularly brilliant points on the sermon.

Activity and a sense of 'needing to get things done' can even enter our devotional time. I remember hearing a preacher urge his listeners to 'spend at least thirty minutes a day in prayer'. Was he right? Well, of course, it's good to have the discipline of a certain time in prayer – but perhaps not if it simply feeds our inner frenzy to find peace by *doing*, to find spirituality by achieving, to find acceptance from God by performing. I have person- ally found Bible-in-a-year resources helpful, yet as I look back on some mornings when I was practically speed- reading in an effort to retrieve a lost day (or on one occa- sion a whole month!), I can't help wondering if this is how life is meant to be. Does it really matter if I read through the Bible *in a year*?

When my friend urged me all those years ago to kick the leaves, there were no mobile phones, yet even then I found it hard to take his advice. But where can I find stillness now? There is nowhere I cannot be reached. If

I cry out along with the psalmist, 'Hide me in the shadow of your wings', even as those wings close in around me, in my pocket is the possibility of a ping that whispers, 'Rob, you've got mail. It could be really important, and unless you take a quick peek, how will you know?'

Someone who has spent a lifetime in Bible teaching told me he believed that the things many preachers speak most passionately about are those that they themselves struggle with. Ah! Now my secret is out. Despite my friend's injunction, I confess that I still find it hard just to kick the leaves, and even in my devotions, I find it so tempting to prove to God that I am worth loving.

The other day, my three-year-old grandson brought me a drawing he had done of a cow. It resembled a bus with no wheels. I heard myself say, 'Wow! That's brilliant!' And as I spoke, a moment of joy flooded my soul as I felt that maybe my father, God, does the same with me. Could it be that when I only manage to read a few verses of the Bible and spend just a couple of minutes in prayer, he looks at me and whispers, 'Brilliant!' Could it really be true that at least with *him* there is nothing to prove?

Now wouldn't that be something?

22

Character Crisis

H OW DO YOU judge a Christian speaker? Is it by their expository skill, their brilliance at telling stories, their understanding of theology, their wit, their wisdom . . .?

A friend of mine who has spent many years running large Christian events told me how the 'techies' – those who look after the sound, the PowerPoints and a dozen other unnoticed things – do *their* judging. She said:

These techies have heard the best speakers from around the world. They've listened to the funny ones and the serious ones. They've heard the jokes, the stories, and the illustrations – often many times over. They judge these speakers, at least in part, by the way they behave towards the team. They could be the best Bible teacher in the history of Christendom, but if they stamp and kick when their mic isn't quite right, if they complain bitterly when somebody makes an occasional mistake with a PowerPoint, and – especially – if they never say a kind word or a simple 'thank you', then even if 10,000 people clap for an hour at the end of their talk, back stage, at least, they're *toast*.

I've thought a lot about my friend's comments and I've come to believe they contain a truth so powerful and disturbing that we often dare not face it. It is this: there is something more important than gift – even *great* gift.

Many of us have heard of the three Cs that it is wise to consider before appointing somebody to any position, whether it's in a multinational company or a local church. They are: competency, chemistry and character. 'Competency' measures how well equipped people are to do the job in hand – their skills if you like. 'Chemistry' measures how easily they will get on with other people. And 'Character' measures the kind of person they *are*.

But which of the three Cs is the most important? Well, it depends. If you are about to have a life-threatening operation, you'd probably settle for the most brilliant surgeon in the world even if he is also the grumpiest person on the planet and robs banks in his spare time.

But although there might be occasional exceptions, the truth is that in almost any area of life good *character* is the most important. Perhaps this quality is best described by the nine qualities that Paul talks about: 'love, joy, peace, patience, kindness, goodness, faithfulness, gentleness [and] self-control' (Galatians 5:22–3, ESV).

It's easy to make huge mistakes about success. Just because somebody is successful in business, it doesn't necessarily make them a good church treasurer, and just because they are a good communicator, it doesn't make them a good leader. If we rush to appoint someone to a position – perhaps being star-struck on 'competence' – we may take a year or so to realise we have chosen somebody who is controlling, difficult to work with, and too used to having their own way. In our churches and Christian organisations, we need to be not only striving for excellence in what we do but emphasising the vital importance of character in how we do it. Honest and open discussion – yes. Rude and cutting emails – no.

In his book *Against the Night: Living in the New Dark Ages*, Chuck Colson painted an apocalyptic view of the crisis at the heart of humanity and suggested a cause:

. . . a crisis of immense proportion is upon us. Not from the threat of nuclear holocaust or a stock market collapse, not from the greenhouse effect or trade deficits . . . Though all these represent serious problems, in the end they alone will not be our undoing.

No, the crisis that threatens us, the force that could topple our monuments and destroy our very foundations, is within ourselves – *the crisis of character.*[*]

I know a couple of techies who would agree with him.

* Charles Colson, *Against the Night: Living in the New Dark Ages* (Vine Books, 1989), p. 12.

23

Seen and Heard

IT WAS THE Mother's Day service at her church. Sarah's stomach was churning as she watched the stewards go down the aisles giving tiny potted plants to every mum. Suddenly one of them appeared at her side and pressed a plant into her hands. She took it clumsily, spilling a little earth on her dress, but then the woman said, 'Oh, sorry, you're not a mum are you?' and took the pot out of her hands.

Sometimes when I hear stories like that I feel truly ashamed of those who caused such hurt, and then I realise that it could so easily have been me who acted so insensitively, me who didn't really know whether leaving the plant was worse than retrieving it, me who just didn't *understand*.

One of the most remarkable pictures of Jesus in the New Testament is of a high priest who *does* understand.

He knows what we are going through. And it is this very Christ who calls us to at least *try* to understand the experiences of others.

Listen to this woman and try to hear not just her words but her heart:

> I didn't tell many people, just a few who promised to pray for me. Not that many people understand that I am grieving. But I am. I am grieving not just for the baby I want, but for lost hopes and dreams. People say you don't miss what you haven't had – but you *do*. It's just a different sort of missing.

If you and I are to truly support those who are experiencing infertility then we will need to grasp how deep this tragedy is for them. One woman described it like this: 'It is a cyclical grief. Every month, you know when it will be at its worst, and you know that the strength you have found today will need to be found again in just a few weeks' time.'

Ann put it like this: 'When we first found out the situation, my husband went into shock. He cried every day for two years.' She then made a telling comment: 'I have shed more tears lately than in the early years.' She and her husband are well into their fifties now, but the pain goes on as they attend the weddings of friends' children and gaze into the prams of grandchildren.

When we understand at least a little, we will never again treat infertility lightly. We may think twice before we 'boast' about our children or grandchildren in front of friends, or perhaps we will stop guessing (often wrongly) why couples do not have children – 'Oh, she was so devoted to her career that she left it too late.' And if we understand, we may be kinder in the way we deal with those who are childless as we announce our own 'good news'. Perhaps we'll be more like the woman who rang her friend and said, 'I know this will be hard for you, so I want to tell you before I tell any of my other friends – and my heart goes out to you.'

Of course, there are sometimes blessings attached to not having children of your own, not least that many people often play a vital role in the lives of the children of others. But if we are to *understand*, then it is not there that we begin: we begin with the pain. Pain such as that experienced by the woman who eventually became pregnant but then had a miscarriage. Her husband said, 'We'd already been shopping for baby things and had put down a deposit on a pram. We never went back for the refund.'

We can't put it right. We can't always get it right. And in spite of all I have said above, we can't even completely understand. But we can try.

24

Teach Us to Pray

WHEN I WAS a young Christian, a man came to our church and gave a talk on prayer. He said, 'Why do you find it hard to spend ten minutes talking with God when you can easily spend an hour talking to your girlfriend?' It struck me then that older people can impart incredible wisdom, but they also have the ability to come out with absolute tosh. I think of two comments my mother made after Claire Tompkinson had finished with me and I was a heartbroken fourteen-year-old. She said, 'Never mind! There are plenty more fish in the sea.' I didn't want lots of other fish – I wanted dolphin Claire. And then she added: 'Anyway, cheer up – we've got jam roly-poly for afters.' My life was over, my love life ruined, and the best comfort she could come up with was jam roly-poly for tea.

But to go back to that visiting preacher, what I wanted to say to him was, 'I can *see* my girlfriend. I can watch her, see her reaction when I say something and hear her replies. *Of course* it's harder to talk with somebody you can't see, can't hear and who – at least in my experience – never answers back so you can physically hear him.'

When I was asked to give a talk entitled 'How to pray', I thought about that occasion when the disciples woke early one morning to find Jesus' sleeping mat already empty. They discovered him praying 'in a solitary place', maybe in the hills above Galilee. Moments like these must have had a deep impact on the disciples. They had attended the synagogue all their lives and had prayed thousands of prayers, but as they watched Jesus praying, they saw something special – something that one day led them to say, 'Teach us to pray.'

If you have lost heart in prayer, then listen to the sheer simplicity of Jesus' teaching: 'When you pray, go into your room [and] close the door' (Matthew 6:6). I suppose the modern equivalent of 'close the door' might be 'switch off your mobile phone'. Next, Jesus says not to worry about the length of our prayers, in contrast to those who think they will be heard for their 'many words'. And then he goes on: 'This, then, is how you should pray; "Our Father in heaven . . ."'

This short prayer, which we have come to know as The Lord's Prayer, begins with the three things that God wants from us: reverence – 'Hallowed be your name'; allegiance – 'Your kingdom come'; and obedience – 'Your will be done.' And then it goes on to ask for the three things we need from God: food – 'Give us today our daily bread'; forgiveness – 'Forgive our sins'; and freedom – 'Deliver us from evil.' This is a prayer for the whole of our lives: our past, our present, our future.

I know some readers will find it easy to pray – perhaps you may even have a special ministry of prayer. But what if you are not one of them? What if, even though you serve God faithfully, you have stopped spending time alone with him in prayer? Is it possible that sometime during this week you could go into a quiet room, close the door and say that simple prayer? Perhaps in your marriage, you and your husband or wife have never really prayed together. Could you begin the day by saying that prayer together from now on? Do you have a good friend with whom you share your deepest joys and fears but never pray together? Could you start to change that by saying the prayer that Jesus taught?

I know it won't take very long to say, and because of the desperate need most of us have to prove ourselves, even to God, it won't feel anything like long enough. But it is a start – and perhaps it will be a lot more than just a start.

After all, it's what *Jesus* taught about prayer.

25

Dare to be Vulnerable

SOMEBODY ONCE SAID that with regard to our children's lives, 'The days are long, but the years are short.' That has certainly been true in my experience, but it's also true in respect of the life of Care for the Family.

It seems as if it was only yesterday when I met with Lyndon Bowring, the chairman of CARE, to talk about starting Care for the Family. I had just resigned as a partner in my legal practice and Lyndon was very instrumental in getting us launched – we began as a department of CARE. I remember well part of the conversation we had that day. 'You and Dianne will be able to tour the country telling people how to build strong marriages,' Lyndon said.

'Ah,' I replied. 'There's a bit of a problem with that.'

Lyndon raised an eyebrow. 'What kind of problem?'

'Well,' I said, 'we've been married for over fifteen years, but we've been through some very tough times – times when we didn't feel much in love.'

Lyndon answered in a heartbeat. 'All right,' he said. 'Then tell people about *that*.' And, so, one of the foundation blocks of Care for the Family was laid: *vulnerability*.

Vulnerability remains one of our core values today. Some time ago, I was addressing twenty people who were interested in speaking on behalf of Care for the Family. This is part of what I said to them:

If you have the perfect marriage, have never had a row, spend most evenings gazing into each other's eyes, and can't wait to share your pearls of wisdom with struggling couples, then you probably aren't our kind of person. And if your children do the washing up every night, complain that church services aren't long enough and ask their teacher for extra homework, and you have already written the first draft of your book *Twelve Steps to Perfect Parenting* for less able parents, then you, too, probably aren't our kind of person. The people we need to work with us are those who have cried a little – or who could, at least, *imagine* crying a little.

A youth leader rang me a few years ago. 'I have thirty teenagers in my youth group,' she said. 'Twenty-nine of them are doing fine, but the mother of one of them has just discovered a marijuana joint in his bedroom.' She paused and then went on: 'The problem is – I'm that mother. Do you think I should give up being a youth leader?' I urged her with all my heart to keep going and told her that the day would surely come when she would sit down with another parent going through that same situation and whisper, 'Me, too.'

I have discovered that whether it's coping with difficult teenagers, dealing with the fall-out from an affair, living with crushing debt, or struggling with other difficult or painful experiences, the first thing people need is often not answers but the realisation that they are not alone.

For that reason, the local church can be a wonderful place to find comfort, support and help. But for this to happen, we have to be prepared to be vulnerable. The Apostle Paul recognised that 'when I am weak, then I am strong' (2 Corinthians 12:10). And that is so because weakness causes us to feel our need of God – and of each other.

The idea is not that we all sit down and depress each other. (I have some sympathy with the atheist who said to the Christian, 'Tell me your certainties. I have enough doubts of my own.') It is rather that, as well as sharing our successes and joys, we also need to allow others to see a little of our pain. When we do this, it can be incredibly freeing for people. It is easier for them to lower their defences a little and share their heart with us.

I know we can't wear our heart on our sleeves with everybody, but none of us, even leaders, need be condemned to what someone has called 'the Sunday lie-in': 'Oh, *fine*, thanks.'

26

Street Pastors

I HAVE JUST BEEN clubbing. I started out at 9.30 on Friday evening and crawled into bed the next morning at five o'clock. Altogether, I hit five pubs and four nightclubs. No, I'm not in the throes of some midlife crisis (or even one a little later than that). I went as an observer with Street Pastors, the organisation whose volunteers go into city centres to assist people who need help, often because of drinking too much alcohol after a night out. Looking back on that amazing seven and a half hours, a couple of thoughts have struck me that I want to share with you.

The first is that Street Pastors is a ministry that has harnessed the time and skills of people of all ages: those in their sixties, seventies and older work alongside twenty-year-olds. It's fascinating to see how effective older people are in this work. I suppose that in addition to any personal skills they might have, they are totally unthreatening. In an age when those with a few years under their belt can easily feel they have little to offer, this is an initiative in which they thrive.

Next, I was staggered at how warmly the street pastors were welcomed – not just by the police and ambulance services but by the door staff at the clubs and, most of all, by those who are being helped. They often said, 'You're from the churches, aren't you?', but there was no cynicism or rejection. On several occasions, people poured out a story of young faith lost, and I perceived that in some there was a longing to find it again. I have no doubt the street pastors' acceptance has been hard won, but they have achieved it armed only with the gift of bottles of water and free flip-flops. (High heels having long since been removed, their wearers find that bare feet are not great when walking on urine-covered pavements littered with broken glass.)

I have two main memories of that night. The first is when our leader's radio crackled into life and we were called to a nightclub. A young man was lying in an upstairs toilet. We got him downstairs and into a wheelchair to take him to an alcohol treatment centre. As we were pushing him there, he suddenly threw the bucket of vomit he was nursing on his lap into the gutter and some of it caught me. He looked up and said, 'You guys don't get paid for this, do you?'

Our team leader said, 'No, we don't.'

He said, 'You must enjoy it!'

I only just stopped myself saying, 'Oh, yes, mate – my life is so miserable that getting a bucket of sick poured over me at one o'clock on a Saturday morning is a real highlight!'

My second memory is vivid in quite another way. We went to help a young woman sitting in the gutter being sick and she thanked my colleague who wiped the vomit from her face and dress. And then one of the team offered her a bottle of water. She reached out to take it and, as he passed it to her, an onlooker said, 'That's a kind thing you're doing.' In that moment, it seemed to me that time went backwards, and I wasn't standing in a modern city street but on a dusty road in ancient Palestine. I almost felt I could hear the young teacher speaking, 'I was thirsty and you gave me something to drink' (Matthew 25:35).

The street pastors will be out again next weekend and they are especially busy on Bank Holidays and at Christmas and New Year. Some people call them 'the Flip-Flop Brigade'.

I call them the hands and feet of Jesus.

27

Why Death is Hard to Live With

I REMEMBER HEARING THE news that Steve Jobs, the founder of Apple, had died. Six years previously, he had given a speech to the graduating class at Stanford University in which he used this quote: 'If you live each day as if it was your last, someday you'll most certainly be right.'

In one of his obituaries, Jobs was called 'the greatest inventor since Eddison'. The devices he created 'saved time' for billions of people around the world as documents, music and ideas could now be transmitted in nanoseconds. Yet the words of Jesus still prove true and, at the very end of Jobs' life, even he could not add to it 'a single hour' (Luke 12:25).

In an age in which we can do things that previous generations could not even have imagined, it seems strange that the power of the final enemy to visit each of us at about the same time as the psalmist suggested so long ago – 'seventy years, or eighty, if our strength endures' (Psalm 90:10) – is undiminished. This old foe seems to have no respect. He calls uninvited, at all hours, and with no thought for our position in society. He asks neither beggar nor billionaire for permission to enter. The old poem 'The Glories of Our Blood and State' by James Shirley puts it well:

> Death lays his icy hand on kings:
> Sceptre and Crown
> Must tumble down,
> And in the dust be equal made
> With the poor crooked scythe and spade.

And yet, common as it is to all men and women, we still find death so hard to live with. C.S. Lewis said of the Christian: 'Of all men, we hope most of death; yet nothing will reconcile us to – well, its *unnaturalness*.'* Perhaps that is why even men and women of strong faith may approach death with trepidation. It is in some ways understandable for us to be afraid, yet Jesus had no fear

* C.S. Lewis, *God in the Dock: Essays on Theology and Ethics* (William B. Eerdmans Publishing Co., 2014).

of the final enemy – in fact, he ruined every funeral he went to. He ruined Jairus' daughter's funeral and the funeral of the young man who was restored to his widowed mother. He even ruined his own. Somebody had come into our world who had power over the last enemy.

The book of Hebrews says a fascinating thing of Jesus: 'By embracing death, taking it into himself, he destroyed the Devil's hold on death and freed all who cower through life, *scared to death of death*' (Hebrews 2:14–15, *The Message*, my italics).

I have a planner on my laptop; it is made up of boxes that each have a date written above it. Every day, I am pulled from one box into another. And each box has no patience with the one before it. At one second past midnight, I am pulled through a door into the next box, and for the next twenty-four hours my life will be played out within its walls.

If I am foolish or simply too preoccupied to reflect, I can believe there is an endless supply of boxes waiting for me. But there is not. And for that reason, I must somehow live my life in the *present* box, grasping the preciousness of *this* moment. I must take time to tell those who matter to me that I love them. I must try to forgive as quickly as possible the hurts that come my way. I must steal some minutes in what is always a busy day to pray and to ponder what will happen in the last box. And this is vital, for although we may find it hard to comprehend our own mortality, both Steve Jobs and the Bible are right: there is a last box. And this one has no doors to lead us into the next day.

The biggest question in the whole universe is this: 'Does that last box have no doors because it is just a coffin and death is the end? Or does it have no doors because it has no walls and death is a beginning?'

28

Next Year, We'll Begin Earlier

I REMEMBER ONE BOXING Day very well indeed. The James Bond film had hardly finished and we hadn't even started to make a curry with the left-over bits of turkey when, in a moment of decisiveness, we made a vow that we would do all of next year's Christmas shopping and write all next year's Christmas cards before the end of January.

This decision was partly born out of a desire to use time more effectively, but to be honest it was mostly a direct result of wrapping socks, aftershave and completely useless 'Christmas gift ideas' at 1.30 a.m. on Christmas morning.

We had spent most of Christmas Eve trudging around shops and buying items in bulk that nobody with an ounce of sense would have wanted even one of. And we kept meeting people who had apparently all conspired earlier to ask us the same question: 'Final bits and pieces, is it?' After several such conversations, I'd practically had to drag Dianne off a dear old lady from church who'd only got as far as 'Final bits . . .'

Twelve hours later in the early hours of Christmas morning, we found ourselves arguing about whose fault it was that fifty cards (all written with the loveliest greetings) were still on the staircase waiting for a surname, house number or, in some cases, the name of a city to be added to the address. And it was as we were sitting on the bedroom floor surrounded by wrapping paper, gift tags and Sellotape that hid its edge like a Scotch tape chameleon, that the seeds of frustration were sown that caused us to make our vow on Boxing Day: 'Next year, we'll begin earlier.'

So we did. We went Christmas shopping on 1 January. As we ambled around the sales, we congratulated ourselves on the bargains we'd found. 'Those bath salts would have cost us £5 before Christmas,' purred Dianne as she got change from 50p. I countered with, 'Look at these cards, "Slightly shop soiled. Various designs. Fifty for a pound."' Like Santa's little helpers, we trundled our booty home – the whole lot obtained for under £75.

Next day, when we started to write the cards, we didn't find it quite so easy. We had to imagine to whom, out of our friends, family and acquaintances we might still be speaking, and then we had to dream up an appropriate greeting. 'Hope you've had another great year!' was risky in case it turned out to be the worst of their lives. After serious deliberation we settled on 'Happy Christmas' (it has a ring to it, don't you think?). But it was so boring. We wrote four cards and turned to the wrapping of presents.

We had only imprisoned one pair of cut-price boxer shorts in bargain wrapping paper when it happened: we started to laugh. We laughed until tears fell on the pack of five ties we'd bought for a fiver and trickled onto the 'gold look' biros we'd had inscribed with the names of various relatives.

And when we stopped laughing we picked everything up – cards, simulated leather wallets, stress-relieving paper weights – bundled them into the back of our wardrobe and decided we weren't going to look at any of it again until at least 1 December.

If we hadn't laughed, we'd have cried – cried that we'd let ourselves get so screwed up about cards that many wouldn't read properly and presents that nobody really needed. And we'd have cried that we'd almost missed again the real meaning of Christmas and the wonder of . . . the Gift.

29

The Room Next Door

WHEN I WAS speaking at a Christian festival once, I asked the audience a question: 'Who's looking forward to going to heaven?' All around the auditorium hundreds of hands went up. Then I asked another question: 'Who'd like to go today?' I have never seen hands descend so quickly!

Of course, there are many reasons for the tension between longing to go to heaven and not wanting to go immediately. But I'm sure that one of these is simply that we don't have an understanding of what the transition will be like. What will happen when we take that last breath?

For over half a century, I'd listened to preachers trying to explain this, but, to be honest, their personal opinions and different interpretations of the Bible produced such varied scenarios that I'd all but given up on any hope of a reliable description. Recently, however, when I was attending a funeral, I heard an illustration that helped me. It is a poem by Canon Scott-Holland that is often read on such occasions. The opening lines are:

> Death is nothing at all.
> I have only slipped away into the next room.

I must admit that I've always found the poem a little too sentimental, but as I sat and considered those words again, I was reminded of an incident that occurred in the last twenty-four hours of Jesus' earthly life. The morning before he died, he asked his disciples to find a room in which he could eat the Passover meal with them. That evening, he told them that he was going to die, and then he said this, 'My Father's house has many rooms . . . I am going there to prepare a place for *you*' (John 14:2, my emphasis). It seemed to me that the image that Jesus used – moving from one room into another – was not so far from that used in the poem.

The philosopher Dallas Willard put it like this:

[A] picture [of death] is of one who walks to a doorway between rooms. While still interacting with those in the room she is leaving, she begins to see and converse with people in a room beyond, who may be totally concealed from those left behind. Before the widespread use of heavy sedation, it was quite common for those keeping watch to observe something like this. The one making the transition often begins to speak to those who have gone before. They come to meet us while we are still in touch with those left behind. The curtain parts for us briefly before we go through.[*]

Because Jesus understood the 'nearness' of that other world, he was able – even as he was dying – to make an appointment with one of the thieves who was hanging on a cross next to him. He promised to meet the thief in a garden later that day: 'Today you will be with me in paradise' (Luke 23:43). The word 'paradise' translates as 'the garden of God'.

Jesus talks about some of those who love him who will not 'taste death' (Mark 9:1). The writer and preacher Peter Marshall illustrated this by describing a child playing in the evening with her toys. Gradually she grows tired and falls asleep, and her mother or father picks her up and takes her to bed. The next thing she experiences

[*] Dallas Willard, *The Divine Conspiracy: Rediscovering Our Hidden Life in God* (HarperCollins, 2014), p. 100.

– 'tastes' – is the light of a new day flooding her bedroom. She remembers neither falling asleep nor going to her bedroom.

I realise there are many theological questions about death to consider, yet the Bible urges us time and time again to let the prospect of the reality of life beyond death affect the way we live now. If we can recognise the 'thinness' between the world we now inhabit and what we call 'heaven', then perhaps we will come to an incredible realisation: the one who has redeemed us stands waiting in the room just beyond that in which we carry on our everyday lives. That room is near – very near.

And if we can grasp that truth, the way we live in that first room will be changed – for ever.

30

Schadenfreude

I AM IN A traffic jam on a motorway. As we inch forward, my friends and I speculate about the cause. We haven't seen any roadworks signs or warnings of an accident ahead, so what can it be? Eventually the road clears and we discover that an accident has happened on the opposite carriageway, and the cause of the delay is simply that drivers on our side are rubbernecking – slowing down to take a look as they pass.

I remember driving by a house that was on fire. The emergency services were there and the scene was chaotic. I pulled my car over and watched with my fellow passengers until one of them said, 'Let's not enjoy somebody else's disaster.' That incident was almost forty years ago, yet I have never forgotten his words.

The Germans have a word to describe this: *schaden-freude*. It means 'pleasure derived by someone from another person's misfortune'. Let me give one more example. While watching the World Cup on TV, I noticed that when a team wins, the camera goes first to its support-ers who are celebrating wildly with hands, drinks – and occasionally people – flying into the air. Then, immedi-ately afterwards, the camera pans to the opposing team's supporters. The sight there is of devastation – people with hands over their faces and shoulders that are slumped and, not infrequently, a small boy in tears being comforted by his father. The producers of sports programmes understand that *schadenfreude* really comes into its own when we are watching the pain of opponents.

I sometimes see *schadenfreude* in the church. Perhaps we hear that a Christian leader has had an affair and we somehow convince ourselves that it is our duty to inform ourselves about it. We scour the web for details and then discuss these with other Christians. Or it may be that a thriving local church (a more 'successful' one than ours!) goes through an almighty split. We quiz for details those who have left, we speculate on what we don't know, and we talk about it – a lot. We may well dress up our various conversations as 'Have you heard the sad news . . .' or 'Let's pray for . . .' or (if we are particularly ungracious), 'Well, let's hope they learn from this', but the truth is that we are just rubberneck-ing. We do it in church, we do it in coffee shops, and we do it on social media.

The Bible says that 'Love does not delight in evil' (1 Corinthians 13:6). Of course, it's not always wrong to talk about these situations – especially if it is part of our responsibility to protect victims, and, after all, we are called to pray for those involved. But we must avoid like the plague an attitude in our hearts that is secretly pleased when those with whom we disagree theologically, those who seem to have known blessing greater than ours, or even those we just don't like, go through troubled times.

We must steer clear of that attitude for at least three reasons. First, so much of this kind of talk is simply gossip, and gossip is like a secret craving; we say we don't want to do it, but when the opportunity arises, we just can't resist. The book of Proverbs puts it like this: 'Rumours are dainty morsels that sink deep into one's heart' (Proverbs 18:8, NLT). And it's not just in the telling: 'Wrongdoers eagerly *listen* to gossip' (Proverbs 17:4, NLT). Second, it's wrong because we are meant to be genuinely hurt when others are hurting – to feel as God feels. In the words of the song, 'Break my heart for what breaks yours'.* And, third, the belief that the

---

* Brooke Fraser, *Hosanna*, Hillsong United.

traumas or failures of others could never be *our* experience is both foolishness and pride. We would all do well to remember that cars on our side of the motorway crash as well.

Sometimes *our* car.

31

Cynicism Corrupts

IMAGINE THAT THE C.S. Lewis character Screwtape had written another letter to his nephew. This time, the senior demon is instructing his nephew on strategies to ensure that even if a child is brought up in a Christian home, their heart will be hard towards God.

I expect an enterprising young devil could think of dozens of weapons that might be effective. 'Doubt' could work, as could 'Criticism from more "mature" Christians forgetting to look at the heart and getting het up over minor issues such as clothing or failure to attend the weekly church Bible study'. Or perhaps 'Sheer boredom' would help make a kid of fifteen believe that if heaven was like church on a Sunday morning – only longer – they'd rather not go there.

Any of those strategies might be useful, but when I was researching a book on what makes it harder for kids to develop a faith of their own, time and time again I came across a more devastating weapon: *cynicism*.

Cynicism is deadly because it slowly chokes the ability to believe, to see God at work and experience the reality of his love and presence. So many young people I spoke with had become cynical of anything to do with Christianity. And, sadly, many of them had 'caught' that cynicism from older Christians – even parents.

It is 1.30 p.m. and your family have just sat down to Sunday lunch. As you are carving the meat, you say to your husband or wife, 'When that woman leads worship she drives me crazy. By the time we'd sung that song five times, I'd lost the will to live.' They reply, 'You were lucky you went out with the kids to their class. The sermon was like stand-up comedy – jokes, stories, Beatles music. The only thing we didn't get was any decent teaching. It wasn't worth listening to.'

The problem with children is sometimes not that they don't listen to us, but that they hear every word. And the message the children get here is that the leaders in their church are either ungodly or fools – perhaps both. One day, aged fifteen, one of them will say, 'I don't want to go any more. The worship is rubbish and the sermons are lame.'

A friend who has attended a large church for many years told me that he and his wife made a vow that to the best of their ability their children would never hear them speak negatively about their church. I asked him how he deals with things he's not happy with. He replied, 'We talk about it privately and if it's serious enough, I go to the leaders. But whenever possible, we speak positively about things.'

And then he said this: 'I want my kids to see church through eyes that look for God at work.'

We should run from cynicism; it is corrosive. And, particularly as a father, I have learnt that the voice of my cynicism will make it harder for my children to hear the voice of God.

32

Abide with Me

As I write, I am in Israel. For the past week, I have been here filming some of the events of Jesus' life for television.

I have been to this fascinating land many times before, but this time I experienced privileges that were new to me. One of these was being alone in the Garden of Gethsemane after we were given permission to film late in the evening. As I sat there, I imagined that night before Jesus died when he must have seen the torches of the soldiers as they made their way up the hill towards the olive grove where he had so often spent time. He said to his disciples, 'Here comes my betrayer!' (Matthew 26:46).

We filmed the story of Bartimaeus, the blind beggar of whom Jesus asked the strange question, 'What do you want me to do for you?' (Mark 10:51). But perhaps his question was not so strange. Perhaps the greatest temptation is to settle for that which is safe, instead of for the desire of our hearts. Bartimaeus could have requested enough money to never need to beg again, but, no, he said, '*I want to see.*' And the first thing he saw was the face of Jesus.

My mind goes back now to Sunday's filming and a long, dusty road. We tried to capture again the events of the day after the crucifixion when two of Jesus' disciples were walking to a small village called Emmaus, about eight miles outside Jerusalem. There is no longer walk than the one away from the grave of somebody you love and from dreams that lie broken, but as the two journeyed, they were joined by a stranger. Later, the couple said that when he spoke with them, it was as if their hearts burned within them.

When they finally reached the village, the stranger seemed as though he would have gone on. But the two disciples said, 'Abide with us: for it is toward evening, and the day is far spent' (Luke 24:29, NKJV). It was this sentence that captured the imagination of a Scottish clergyman, Henry Francis Lyte, who wrote the hymn 'Abide with Me' three weeks before he died of tuberculosis.

The man agreed to stay with the two disciples and later that evening they sat to eat together. And that's when it happened: the disciples asked the stranger if he would bless the bread, and when he broke it – as they had seen him do so many times before – it was as if their eyes were opened. They saw *him*.

When we finished filming and the crew was packing up, I ambled along the road, a question going through my head. Was there a reason why Jesus seemed as if, perhaps, he *wouldn't* stay with them? Why he would have gone on alone?

The only answer I could find was the obvious one – that at the heart of every relationship is the need to know you are truly wanted. But find the answer or not, I couldn't get that incident out of my mind, and later in the week it came back to me as I looked over Galilee from the Eastern side on the Golan Heights. The lake sat in a great bowl beneath me, but just a few miles in the other direction were the lights of Syria. A few nights before, we'd heard the sound of armaments and seen flashes in the sky. And as I thought about the challenges we face as nations, families and individuals, I felt an overwhelming need of his presence, and I caught myself whispering under my breath, 'No, don't go on – stay.'

'Help of the helpless, O abide with me.'

33

You Can't Fix Everything

'IN SOOTH, I know not why I am so sad . . .' so begins *The Merchant of Venice*. Do you ever talk to yourself? It's not entirely unbiblical. In an earlier chapter, I've mentioned how David sometimes did this in the Psalms. On three occasions he asked himself why he was so discouraged and sad (Psalm 42:5, 11; 43:5).

I'm sure there are many reasons why we may feel downcast, but I'm convinced that one of them is that there is so much heartache in the world and we feel that, somehow, it's our responsibility to sort it out.

The cause is, perhaps, due to our personality; we have a soft heart and are troubled by the pain of others. We watch the TV pictures of children caught up in wars and famines. We feel anxious and burdened, weighed down with the pressure of our inability to stop the suffering. In many ways, those responses are good; soft hearts are nearer to God's heart than hard ones. The problem comes when we cross the line of Christ-like compassion and believe that it's our task to put it right – *all of it*. When we can't do that, we feel crushed by guilt because we have let people down.

But you and I cannot bear the pain of the whole world – not the pain of the child in Sudan, the pain of the young couple in our church who have just lost a child, or the pain of a church being driven apart by argument and wrangling.

Professor Lewis Smedes had a name for this nagging guilt that robs our soul of peace and joy if it is left unchecked. He calls it, 'the demon of total accountability'.* Total accountability distorts our compassion and sometimes, mixing in a little pride, causes us to imagine that we can bear a load on our small shoulders that only Jesus can bear. We must be free of it.

Of course, we must care for the needs of others, but, ironically, total accountability often leads to total inaction. It makes us believe that because the problem is so overwhelming, there is nothing we can do to make a difference. And that inaction gnaws at our very soul. But

* Rob Parsons, *The Book That Changed My Life*: '*How Can It Be All Right When Everything is All Wrong*' *by Lewes B. Smedes* (Authentic, 2011).

this response is almost always wrong. We cannot bear *all* the pain, and we cannot put it *all* right, but we can make it just a little easier for *somebody*.

Maybe we cannot put an end to the church in-fighting – which may well result in another 'split' and all the damage that accompanies it. But we can try to be a peacemaker in some small way, perhaps by bringing a perspective of how pathetically small the 'big issues' may look in ten years' time, let alone from the vantage point of another world.

And we cannot give the child back to the couple who are grieving. But instead of avoiding them in church, we can speak to them for a few minutes. They will forgive our fumbling over the right words, but what will pierce their hearts is when, a year later, nobody mentions their son because people believe 'it's time to move on' and 'time heals'. Time doesn't heal – it's not meant to. We can be the one to give them permission, even years afterwards, to speak about the grief that sometimes still comes back in waves.

The young boy on the hillside in Palestine knew that he couldn't possibly feed 5,000 people. But he did have enough food for one, so he gave that to Jesus and trusted him to do the rest. We can do *something*. No matter how small the amount, we can give regularly to organisations that feed the hungry. And when we see the pain on the television, we can whisper under our breath, 'Lord, use what I give to bring hope in this situation.'

A wonderful story is told about Pope John XXIII when a very intense cardinal was pressurising him to do something about the multiple tragedies in the world. The pontiff told the cardinal that he, too, often experienced the temptation to accept responsibility for the whole world, but he had been helped by an angel who sometimes visited him in the papal bedroom. On one occasion, as he was tossing and turning and feeling responsible for putting right the ills of all mankind, the angel said, 'Hey there, Johnny boy. Don't take yourself so seriously!'

I know full well that selfishness is rife. And I realise that many of us need to be more challenged, more stirred to action, more convicted about the needs of others. But there are some – and perhaps we are one of them – who need the Pope's angel to pay a visit.

34

School Reports

I HAVE JUST BEEN sifting through a box filled with memorabilia from my childhood. Among the assorted items, there is a cycling proficiency certificate. It proved that I could successfully weave between cones in a school playground, but, sadly, not that I could manage to miss crashing into the back of a number 4 bus just six days later. Another certificate assures anybody about to drown that I, as a teenager, was awarded a Bronze Medallion by the Royal Life Saving Society UK. I've never been called upon to use this skill in lifesaving but have often imagined myself laboriously swimming out to sea towards some unfortunate man going under for the third time while yelling to him, 'Don't worry! I'm a bronze medallion lifesaver.' The poor soul could be forgiven for thinking, 'Bronze? I'd better keep waving!'

But it's another item that always takes most of my attention: my school report book, signed every term by my form teacher, W.P. Lewis, BA (I won't tell you what my friend Brian said the 'BA' stood for). Even now, over half a century after W.P. Lewis, BA, wrote 'He is making no use of what little ability he has', that book still has the ability to make my stomach churn. I wasn't any good at school and my report book is full of minor (even if unintended) cruelties. My PE teacher wrote 'Good' in one year's Easter report – then crossed it out and replaced it with 'Satisfactory'. Why would you bother to do that? Did anybody really care whether my effort to leap over a huge wooden horse was in that category or the other?

One of the hardest things to do in my Christian life has been to throw off the sneaking suspicion that in spite of all the talk of his love and grace, God is actually rather like W.P. Lewis, BA. If he is, then it's not hard to imagine my celestial report:

Prayer: Weak. Robert tries hard to pray, but often he just doesn't know what to say and lets his mind wander.

Personal witnessing: Poor. Robert's attempts to turn bus-stop conversations around to the second coming are embarrassing.

Theological knowledge: Patchy. He still can't really explain the problem of suffering.

But God isn't like my old form teacher. He isn't marking me out of 100 and formulating appropriate comments. He isn't itching to write 'Could do better' over my life.

The Apostle Paul says a remarkable thing about God: he is *for* me. He is on my side (Romans 8). Sometimes I wake too early; it's still dark and a voice whispers in my ear, 'If people really knew you, they wouldn't come to hear you speak or buy your books. You're a bit of a hypocrite, Rob. You don't pray enough, read the Bible enough . . .' But then, so often, I hear a voice in my other ear:

I know you. I know you better than you know yourself. I'm not as impressed with the books and speaking events as you appear to be, but I still love you. Nothing you do can make me love you more; nothing you do can make me love you less.

I am so encouraged as I see how Jesus dealt with Peter. Imagine Peter's mother getting his school reports:

Dear Mrs Levi, I'm sorry to tell you that Peter nearly drowned today trying to walk on the lake.

Dear Mrs Levi, I regret to inform you that Peter almost ruined the Transfiguration with a silly comment on the mountain.

Dear Mrs Levi, I have to tell you that Peter cut somebody's ear off in the garden last night.

Dear Mrs Levi, Peter denied the Master today.

But Jesus wasn't like my old form teacher. He saw what Peter could become – somebody who could change the world. He knew what every good parent and teacher knows: *don't read a child's school report as though it is a prophecy of their future life.*

35

Healing in the Local Church

WHEN I WAS a child, I would sometimes say to my mother, 'There's something I want to tell you, but don't go potty with me.' I feel a bit like saying that to you now. I'm honestly not looking for a fight or to churn up dissension. It's just that there's something that's been bothering me for years, and I think it may be time for me to share it.

Let me paint the scenario for you. A member of your church becomes ill – let's say, for the purpose of this chapter, that they are actually diagnosed as terminally ill. Soon the church is doing what it often does so well: cooking meals, running errands and other pastoral care, and praying for the person to be healed. I believe that this is how it should be. We are meant to 'carry each other's burdens' (Galatians 6:2), and I believe that God heals people in response to prayer.

The next step is often that a small group of people agree to meet regularly to pray for the person to be made well. These faithful individuals never miss a Monday evening's prayer session. I thank God for people who are prepared to do that. But here's my dilemma; I'll try my best to explain it as clearly as I can. The meetings go on from week to week, then one day somebody declares that God has revealed to them that the person is going to be healed – perhaps, even, that they are *already* healed. It's not hard to see why some members of the group, and, of course, the person being prayed for, will grasp that declaration with both hands. Or perhaps something else happens. A Christian leader who is well known for their healing ministry gets to hear of the situation and sends word to the church that God is going to heal the person. The crucial point about these declarations, whether made from within the local church or outside it, is that they are unequivocal: 'This person will be well.'

Then the person dies.

The next steps are predictable. There is a sense of embarrassment, a quiet shuffling of feet, and an unspoken agreement not to ask the question on everybody's lips. Sometimes there may be a suggestion that the outcome was affected by those who did not have enough faith. It may be that some of those who prayed never recover from what they believe has happened: God has broken his promise or, perhaps worse, he has been unable or unwilling to heal. Those from outside the local church who declared the healing do not normally offer reasons why they made a mistake on this occasion. In that sense, there is no accountability. I have known some churches repeat this cycle, with intervals of a couple of years, time after time.

Some may say, 'Well, what's wrong with that? After all, the sick person wanted prayer and God may have healed them.' I think that what is wrong is the proclamation of *certainty* that God will definitely heal the person. That 'certainty' has the ability to wreck people's faith when it turns sour. It can lay false guilt on the shoulders of some who may believe that if only they had prayed more or believed more, all would be well. And in terms of relationships and their personal affairs, it may even sometimes prevent a person from approaching death in a helpful way.

If I get sick, please pray for me. If any of you have a particular healing ministry and are willing to pray for me, I will be grateful. It really isn't that I believe God does not perform miracles today. It's just that I know that he doesn't *always* do it, and I want us to still love him, trust him and look after each other when we are disappointed.

Well there it is – my nagging concern out in the open. Forgive me if I have offended you, and especially if I have made it harder for any sick person to believe that God can heal them. He can – *today*. But I thought it was, at least, worth talking about.

Just don't go potty with me.

36

Coping with the Cold War

I WONDER IF, LIKE Dianne and me, you were given these words of advice when you got married: 'Don't let the sun go down on your wrath.' Or, as somebody has paraphrased it, 'Resolve the flack before you hit the sack!' It means that we shouldn't go to bed not talking, with hurts still festering.

In our marriage, I think that in general we have striven to do that, although Dianne confesses she is much worse than me about making up quickly when we've had a row. We go to bed not talking and she simply will not give in. We lie there, back to back, huffing and puffing and pulling at the duvet, convinced that the other one has got more than their fair share of it. We always say a short prayer before we go to sleep, but it's hard to talk to God when you're not talking to each other. In fact, I can practically feel Dianne trying desperately to resist the temptation to say, 'God, please help Rob to be more gracious when he's in the wrong!'

But we still won't be speaking and the disagreement will still be nowhere near to getting resolved until, after what seems like hours, one of us makes the first move and mumbles, 'I'm sorry.' After that, we'll begin to talk and normally we find that the whole argument had got out of proportion. Poor communication was partly to blame and, together with a dose of selfishness and a touch of pride, before we knew it – conflict!

Even if it takes us until the early hours of the morning, we've learnt that it's best to try to sort things out straight away. The incredible thing about rows in marriage is that if you resolve them quickly, two days later it's likely that you won't even remember what the fuss was about. But if you don't sort them out, the bitterness can stay with you down the years.

It's not unusual to find marriages where the couples have absolutely no mechanism to resolve even the simplest conflict. They go through twenty-plus years of married life sleeping back to back, huffing and puffing and pulling at the duvet and thinking: 'I won't give in on this', 'It's up to him/her to make the first move', 'I'm not going to be the one to lose face.'

We've all heard the reasons people give for separating. Often the causes are summarised by phrases such as 'We just can't live together' or 'We don't love each other any more.' But I can't help feeling that behind the big, weighty issues there are actually hundreds of small areas of conflict that were never resolved and were left to fester down the years.

Resolving conflict means letting the other person know that they've hurt us or that what they are doing is driving us bananas. It's a misconception that we should always take hurt on the chin and never let anybody know about it. Reconciliation and forgiveness demand openness.

I remember asking Dianne a question when the kids were young: 'Darling, if you could change anything about me, what would it be?'

She didn't even hesitate. 'When you finish shaving, I'd like you to wipe the stubble from the sink.' Then she added, 'I don't know how you do it, but you manage to get the shaving foam up the wall, above head height. I'd like you to wipe it off. And instead of rolling the wet towel in a ball and throwing it in the bath, I'd be grateful if you would fold it and put it over the radiator.'

'Is that it?' I said.

She smiled. 'Rob, that will do for starters!'

It was a revelation to me. Then Di explained. 'I'm a home maker. That's my job right now. And when you and the kids leave the place as if Hurricane Katrina had hit us, the message you give me is that the job I do doesn't matter – and that hurts.'

You may be reading this and thinking, 'I wish the only problem we had in our marriage was a bit of stubble around the sink!' Well, Di and I have had bigger issues too, but we're convinced that the way to settle the serious disagreements is to learn to deal with the simple things that can irritate, dissatisfy or disappoint us. Conflicts like these love to remain unresolved and cluster together in our minds until frustration turns to dislike, and dislike perhaps even to hate. We need to sort them out *now*.

CHECKLIST

- Don't be too proud to be the first to give in.
- Tell each other how you feel.
- Winning isn't everything – particularly if you're the one who is always good with words – because the other person will still be bitter. Back off a little and hear what the other is saying.
- 'Resolve the flack before you hit the sack.' Agree between you to try hard never to go to bed still feeling angry with each other.

37

Songs of Innocence or Experience?

WHEN I WAS a teenager, I went to the little Gospel Hall on the corner of my street. The church of my youth had lots of things going for it, but excitement wasn't one of them. And it was in search of a little excitement that my friend Carl and I occasionally used to desert our Brethren assembly and sneak into the large Pentecostal church in the heart of our city. If the elders from our church had caught us within fifty yards of the place we'd have been excommunicated at least, but the second we walked through the doors of the City Temple, Carl and I knew it was worth the risk. We were always wide-eyed.

Whereas our little place of worship had pews, the Pentecostals had cinema seats; and whereas we had 100 members, they had 1,000 – which meant the variety of 'sisters' was truly awesome. And in the Temple, there was always the chance of seeing or hearing something amazing. I remember Carl leaning into me and whispering, 'Listen, I think they're going to do it.' I listened and suddenly someone started praying out loud in a language I thought I'd heard in our local ice cream parlour. I whispered, 'He sounds like Mr Rabbiotti when he's shouting at his wife.' Carl allowed himself one of his superior smiles and said, 'It's tongues – it's the language of heaven.'

Someone once said, 'As you get older, you are more likely to remember something in your childhood than where you left your glasses!' I think that's right, and when it comes to the City Temple, it's the singing especially that I remember with crystal clarity. They sang loudly, they sang enthusiastically, and the songs were so positive. My favourite was 'Count Your Blessings' – 'Count your blessings, name them one by one, and it will surprise you what the Lord has done.'

One day the pastor spoke about that song and told us it was a sin to take God for granted. He said that God liked us to be grateful and that Jesus was really disappointed that only one leper came back to say thank you. He told us to make sure that we thanked God every day for the good things he has given us.

I loved singing 'Count Your Blessings' but adulthood robbed me of that joy. Cynicism picked at the words, sophistication complained about the melody, and there were plenty of people ready to tell me that life wasn't quite so simple, that pain was everywhere, and that silly, shallow songs had no place in a mature Christian's musical repertoire.

So I stopped singing my favourite song and instead I chose one called, 'Count Your Problems, Name Them One By One'. Even during times when I was spared major traumas, I'd find smaller ones that seemed worth counting. Last year my central heating packed in for two days. Last month I lost my mobile phone. Last week the courier delivered some books I'd ordered to the wrong address and I had to spend an hour on the phone trying to find them.

When I was forty years old, I went to Africa. I saw shanty towns where tens of thousands of people live with no running water and no proper sewage system. Often a family of six live in a room just ten feet by ten with a few planks of wood for walls and a bit of tin for a roof. Some are hungry and some have AIDS, and all of them would give almost anything to live in a house where the central heating broke down once in a while.

As I'm writing, my eyes are filling with tears, and I ask God to forgive the sheer selfishness of my little world and the breathtaking lack of gratitude I have shown him for all his many mercies to me. And I make a vow:

I'm going to start singing the old song again.

38

At Least

MY FRIEND LOST a child. It wasn't after a long illness and there was no chance to say goodbye or to whisper a last 'I love you'. No, it was due to a car accident that took just thirty seconds from beginning to end and changed the lives of a family for ever. I remember my friend telling me what life was like in the weeks and months after his son's death. He said that one of the hardest things to deal with were the comments of Christians who said things like, 'But at least you've got three other lovely children.' He told me, 'I would gaze at them and say, "I know. But I want *him*."'

To be honest, I'd forgotten about the destructive power of those two words *at least* when they are spoken in such a situation, but then I listened to a programme where church leaders Rick and Kay Warren talked about their son's suicide. Kay echoed my friend's experience; she said how hurtful it was when people tried to somehow make it all better with the use of those same two words: '*At least* you know where he is', '*At least* you've got each other', '*At least* . . .'

Of course, we often just don't know what to say to those experiencing such pain, but I wonder if sometimes we feel a responsibility to defend God – to search for a positive comment that will bring some meaning into the situation. When I was speaking with a woman whose young husband had died, she said that one of the hardest things to deal with was the sense of betrayal by God that her children had felt when it happened. After all, she'd taught them from birth that God loved them all dearly and could do anything, so why didn't he heal their father? She told me how the children had learnt some deep lessons in this area and that they'd eventually come to a place where they were able to begin to trust God again. She also said that the children's battle with God was easier to deal with than some of the comments of Christian friends who seemed determined to provide explanations. They said things like 'All things work together for good – one day you will see the plan', and 'He's in a better place now.' And once again those two words came up: '*At least* you're young – you can marry again', '*At least* you've got the children.'

The incredible thing is that often those who are actually going through these situations are not looking for answers. I was once involved in a debate on the subject of why God allows suffering. Halfway through, it was interrupted by a man in a wheelchair. He had cerebral palsy. He took a long time to communicate what was on his heart, and his speech was hard to decipher, but he repeated it for us: 'People look at me and say "Why?" I look up at heaven and say, "Why not?"' The debate all but ground to a halt.

We need to walk humbly in this area. If people are questioning why tragedy has come into their lives, it's no shame to say: 'I don't really understand why this has happened to you.' In one of the oldest books in the Bible, Job questions God as to why. But then God begins to question Job:

'Have you ever given orders to the morning or shown the dawn its place? . . . Have the gates of death been shown to you? . . . Tell me, if you know all this . . .

'What is the way to the abode of light? And where does the darkness reside? . . . Surely you know, for you were already born! You have lived so many years! . . .'

The LORD said to Job: . . . 'Let him who accuses God answer him!'

Then Job answered the LORD: . . . 'I am unworthy – how can I reply to you? I put my hand over my mouth . . . I will say no more.'

(Job 38:12–21; 40:1–5)

There have been times when I wished I'd done the same.

39

It's Just Jesus

I WAS IN MY twenties and had gone into a small Christian bookshop to buy a Bible. A silver-haired woman, who looked remarkably like pictures I'd seen of the missionary Gladys Aylward, was helping me. She had shown me a number of translations – the *King James*, the *Good News Bible*, *The Living Bible*, the *American Standard Version* and several others – but I just couldn't make up my mind which to have. Eventually (after deciding to ignore the comments of one of the elders of my childhood church who used to say, 'If it was good enough for Saint Paul, then it's good enough for me!'), I pointed to one of the newer translations and said a trifle sniffily, 'I'll take that one please.'

The next thing was to decide what kind of cover to have. Should I go for hardboard, soft cover, or really push the boat out and plump for leather? I chose leather. But now there was another choice to make: the colour. The Gladys lookalike was incredibly patient. She opened boxes containing red, white and black Bibles. I debated and dithered; I delayed and deliberated. Finally, I went for . . . black.

And then I said eight words that for some reason caused Gladys to totally lose it: 'Could you show me some that zip up?' Gladys pushed all the Bibles to one side (not an easy task – by now we were both up to our eyes in Holy Writ) and then she spoke. Her tone of voice was rather different to the one I'd heard up until then; it was low and menacing. 'Young man, all over the world there are believers with practically no access at all to this precious book. If they happen to get a Bible, they share it, sometimes carefully tearing the pages out to be passed around a community.' She stopped briefly to fix me with her eyes and then said, 'Pick one.' I picked.

I hurried from the shop with my new black (zipless) Bible under my arm, feeling chastised. But I have never forgotten that experience because in my heart I knew she was right. In my world, Bibles were everywhere, and I had begun to take this incredible book for granted.

Taking for granted things that are meant to inspire gratitude and awe can come all too easily. Perhaps we regularly say of the Sunday service in our local church, 'I just don't get anything out of it.' I know I have. But in a world where many Christians pay an enormous price for daring to try to meet together, is it possible that we are forgetting what an incredible privilege we have? Was there really nothing at all in the whole service that could have helped us worship God, or encouraged us a little in our walk with him? And even if there wasn't, was there nobody in the entire place to whom we could have spoken in a way that would encourage them or bring them hope? Rick Warren was right when he chose that incredible sentence to start his bestselling book, *The Purpose Driven Life*: 'It's not about you.'

There is no doubt in my mind that taking the Bible and the local church for granted is wrong. But there is another attitude that is much more dangerous: it is *to take Jesus for granted*. It happened to the people of Jesus' hometown, Nazareth. They just got too used to having him around. They said under their breath: 'He's only the carpenter; he fixed my door', 'Look, there's his sister going down the street now', 'Oh, we've known him for ever. *It's just Jesus.*' And because of that – because they took Jesus for granted – a terrible thing happened to them: they missed the power and the glory of the person he really was. The Bible says, 'He could do no mighty work there . . . because of their unbelief' (Mark 6:5,6 ESV). Because of that attitude, their sick stayed sick, their dead stayed dead, and their blind never did see again.

How can we, perhaps especially those of us who have been Christians for decades, avoid the dreadful danger of taking Jesus for granted? Let me share one way. Someone once said, 'If you want to know how much you love something or somebody then imagine it gone forever.' Sometimes I try to imagine Jesus gone from my life. No one to hear the prayers that even I find it easy to pray when I am in great need. No one to lift me up and dust me down when I fall. No meaning in this life and no hope to come.

When I think of that, I have an ache in my very soul. And sometimes I feel like taking my shoes off because I know I am on holy ground, and I feel like crying out:

Lord, forgive me if, by knowing you for so long, I have somehow begun to take you for granted. Forgive me if I have ever allowed for a moment you, the risen Christ of God, to be so diminished by familiarity that I have treated you as though . . . it's just Jesus.

40

One Person

HOW CAN ONE person do so much damage in a local church? I've spoken with many church leaders over the years whose church is going through a tumultuous time, and so often they say that it seems that just *one* dissatisfied person is at the heart of the problem. And whether the church is in Borneo or Balham, some characteristics of this 'one person' seem to be repeated over and over again.

First, they have often come from another church where they were also dissatisfied. A church leader described one such couple in his church: 'When they joined us, they said, "Oh, this church is a breath of fresh air. The worship in our old church was so stilted." But they hadn't been with us more than a year before they were pining for Egypt!' The truth is that if somebody has a couple of churches behind them where they have been unhappy, the chance of yours pleasing them is slight. It might be best not to be taken in by their initial flattery and to encourage them to go back to their old church immediately!

Second, the dissatisfied person may dress it up as healthy discussion, but often they are simply involved in old-fashioned gossip. Typically, they will say to the church leader, 'Lots of us are worried about X or Y.'

The leader will ask, 'Who else is it who feels like this?'

'Ah,' comes the reply, 'I can't give you names.'

Another characteristic is that the issues they articulate as troubling them are often not the real ones. A member complained to a church leader, 'The teaching at this church is too shallow – people are dying spiritually because they are not being fed.' Really? Of course, if the teaching is poor it has to be addressed, but 'dying . . . because they are not being fed'? Even if the teaching is the worst on the planet, we live in a culture where, thanks to modern technology, we can listen to some of the finest Bible teaching from around the world. No need to die spiritually.

Churches argue over four things: the style of worship, the building, the youth work and the style of leadership. When the New Testament writers gave advice to local churches, they knew there would be relationship conflicts

– that's normal. We can be robust in our discussions, but we also have to treat each other with respect and grace. However, they also talked of situations that should *not* be tolerated as normal. Paul said that when people are 'divisive' and they won't change their ways, 'have nothing to do with them' (Titus 3:10). In other words, don't join a little group of discontents. James put it like this: 'Don't bad-mouth each other, friends. It's God's Word, his Message, his Royal Rule, that takes a beating in that kind of talk. You're supposed to be honouring the Message, not writing graffiti all over it' (James 4:11, *The Message*).

The final characteristic of the 'one person' is that often they leave to start a church of their own. And all goes well for a while until one Sunday, someone in their congregation says to them, 'Lots of us are worried about . . .'

41

Deal or No Deal?

LISTEN IN TO Bart Simpson's prayer life. It's Christmas Eve. 'O God, if you bring me lots of good stuff tomorrow, I promise not to do anything bad between now and when I wake up.'

Bart's deal with God may make us smile, but it may make us think as well. Could it be that unwittingly we are living our lives with the unspoken belief that we have a secret 'deal' with God? It goes something like this:

God, I will follow you, serve and love you, but in return you will look after me. A little pain, some persecution that doesn't get too nasty, and minor family traumas are all accepted as part of my sanctification. But that's it. No failing marriages, children who turn their backs on church, illnesses that kill those I love, or redundancies that don't ultimately lead to a more fulfilling job.

I remember a man in his mid-forties. He had been a Christian for years and had seemed to live a charmed life. He had a lovely home, a wonderful family, was financially secure and had been given talent in abundance. Tom was good at everything. Then one day he was made redundant. But his job wasn't the only thing he lost that day. Tom lost his faith in God. He has never been inside a church since. He said to a friend, 'If there is a God who loves me, he wouldn't have let this happen to me.'

Don't be too hard on him. You and I may not know how we will react when we experience what one theologian referred to as 'the seeming betrayal of God'. The theme of the 'deal' is, of course, at the heart of the drama in the oldest book in the Bible: how will Job's love for God hold up when it seems that God is not keeping his end of the bargain?

I suppose it's in the book of Habakkuk that we find the most eloquent summary of the idea of holding on to faith in God when life turns bad on us:

Though the fig-tree does not bud and there are no grapes on the vines, though the olive crop fails and the fields produce no food, though there are no sheep in the pen and no cattle in the stalls, yet I will rejoice in the LORD, I will be joyful in God my Saviour. (Habakkuk 3:17–18)

I find it hard to read that passage because it makes me ask myself whether I love God like that. Secretly, do I only love him if he seems to be 'good' to me?

There's a story that during the Second World War, when a whole nation was praying for deliverance but humanly speaking all seemed lost, an officer sent a message from the beaches at Dunkirk to British military headquarters. It contained just three words, 'But if not'. Apparently, Churchill recognised the biblical reference. This Christian officer was choosing to stand with Job, with Habakkuk, and with three young men who, when faced with death by fire, had said:

King Nebuchadnezzar ... If we are thrown into the blazing furnace, the God we serve is able to deliver us from it ... *But even if he does not*, we want you to know, Your Majesty, that we will not serve your gods or worship the image of gold you have set up. (Daniel 3:16–18, my emphasis)

Don't get me wrong – I'm not looking for trouble. Even just reading the book of Job scares me. And I suppose the truth is that I'd prefer there *was* a deal – to keep my family from harm, my body from illness, my ministry blessed and my critics at bay. But in my heart, I know that real love doesn't operate on the basis of a deal, and I hear myself whisper, as quietly as possible lest he hear and test me:

'But if not . . .'

42

I Will See Him Again

THIS MORNING, AS I was about to rush out of the house, Dianne called out, 'Have you got a minute? I'm in the lounge.'

I popped my head around the door and said (a bit reluctantly), 'Yes, sure. What is it?'

She replied, 'Sit down for a minute and listen to this.'

Dianne had been reading the Bible and something had struck her that she wanted to share with me. Now I've been here before and, normally, if God has spoken to somebody and they want to tell you about it, when they do, it doesn't have the same impact on you as it did on them. The best you can offer is a lame, 'That's wonderful.' But this time it was different.

She was reading about Mary visiting the tomb of Jesus. The story ends well: the risen Christ speaks Mary's name and suddenly she recognises him. But the part Dianne read to me came before that. John 20:13 says that Mary stood outside the tomb, crying. As she wept, she looked in and saw two angels. They asked her, 'Why are you crying?'

She answered, 'They have taken my Lord away and I don't know where they have put him.'

As Dianne read those words to me, I realised that this is how I've often felt myself. There have been times when the lack of the sense of Jesus' presence in my life has been my fault. I remember a well-known Christian leader challenging a group of other leaders who had gathered to pray, myself among them. He related the incident in Luke chapter 2 when Joseph and Mary took the child Jesus to Jerusalem. When the feast was over, they made their way back home to Nazareth. The Bible tells us that they went a day's journey, but didn't realise that Jesus wasn't with them. He said:

That is a danger for somebody in this room. You are pressing ahead in Christian service with lots of exciting programmes, strategies and initiatives. You are busy preaching, organising and pastoring. The only problem is that, somehow, you've managed to leave Jesus behind: you're on your own.

As I heard Di reading those words this morning, I knew that was not how it was for Mary. Mary loved Jesus; she wanted his presence more than anything. While the men were locked away 'for fear of the Jewish leaders' (John 20:19), she was out there – even now Jesus was dead – risking her life for him. But even for people like Mary, who love so much, the living presence of Jesus can sometimes fade.

When I've experienced this myself, I've often not been sure why it has happened. There wasn't a particular sin or attitude that could explain it, no great intellectual doubts had battered my heart, and I wasn't about to walk away from God. It was just that I'd hit a time in my life when it seemed that Jesus wasn't there. It was as if somebody had taken him away and I didn't know where to start looking for him.

I know that you may be able to tell me where to start looking. You might suggest some spiritual disciplines, or perhaps an examination of my motives in my ministry. You could recommend a good book or a DVD of a talk from Spring Harvest, New Wine or Keswick. I know that all or any one of those things may help. But I have come to believe in the mystery of all of this. I have come to believe in the truth that sometimes human beings find it hard to recognise God, even when he is standing in front of them, and that they need a little help.

My real hope – my best hope and, at times, my *only* hope – is that one morning, as unexpectedly as I felt the loss of his presence, I will, in a moment, sense him there and see him again as Mary did and hear his voice as he whispers a name. My name.

43

Handling Criticism

I HAVE RECEIVED MANY letters that made me feel sad, but one in particular stands out. It was from a woman who wrote, 'I have spent fifty years – half a century – imprisoned by other people's opinions of me.' She's not alone.

As a society, we are becoming more critical and the church is no exception. It's true that criticism is often dressed up a little, perhaps prefaced with, 'I've got something I want to say to you in love . . .', but there's still no shortage of those who are ready to tell us what they think. It could be about the colour of your hair, the kind of car you drive or the way your kids behave in church. If you're a church leader it might be a comment from somebody who says they are worried about the youth work/the length of your sermons/the organ/the band.

Your critic may even add the killer blow: 'And I'm not the only one in the church who's worried about this!'

Criticism is hard to take and we shouldn't dismiss it out of hand, but it's vital to distinguish between two kinds of critic. First, there are those who criticise in order to help us. The Bible says, 'Faithful are the wounds of a friend' (Proverbs 27:6, NKJV). Many years ago, my friend Lyndon Bowring came to listen to me speak. He was very encouraging but he also gave me a little advice: 'You spoke too long, Rob. When somebody asks you to speak for thirty minutes, just take twenty-five. I know that sometimes people say to you at the end of your talks, "I could have listened to you all day", but they don't mean it!' Ah, those faithful wounds!

But there is another kind of critic. These people do not have your good at heart. They are not on your side. The purpose of their criticism is not to lift you to better things, but to hurt you. And they often have hidden agendas that make it impossible to please them. A vicar said to me recently, 'A woman sent me a letter that identified thirty things that were wrong with the church. I wrote back and answered every one of the issues she raised.'

I told him I didn't think that had been a good idea. He asked why and I said, 'Because she wasn't satisfied, was she?'

He smiled ruefully. 'No – she's just sent me another list!'

It's not even just a matter of identifying the two kinds of critics and then listening to one and dismissing the other. Much as we hate to admit it, we can often learn something even from those who criticise us with bad motives, for there's sometimes a grain of truth in what they say. So how do we proceed? Paul gave us some clues:

> I care very little if I am judged by you or by any human court; indeed, I do not even judge myself. My conscience is clear, but that does not make me innocent. It is the Lord who judges me . . . He will bring to light what is hidden in darkness and will expose the motives of the heart. At that time, each will receive their praise from God. (1 Corinthians 4:3–5)

In other words:

> I will listen to you – but I won't spend my life wondering what you make of me. I'll listen to my own heart – but even then I'll realise that I can sometimes be a critic who gets it wrong. And that will leave me with a third critic waiting in the

wings – one who knows me better than I know myself, wants me to change, but is *passionate* for my good.

Now there's a critic worth listening to.

44

An Old Lady Sings

JUST BEFORE CHRISTMAS some years ago, I visited a friend in hospital. As I sat by his bed and chatted to him, I heard a strange sound coming from across the aisle. An elderly woman suffering from senile dementia had started to sing, 'O come, all ye faithful' at the top of her voice. It sounded tuneless and shrill. Members of her family who were sitting with her looked embarrassed and tried to get her to stop, but this only resulted in her singing even louder. And then another visitor suddenly made his way to the lady's side. He began to sing with her. Slowly, her relatives started to join in and within moments she was leading the whole ward in that lovely carol.

Later on, when I thought about how embarrassed and uncomfortable we'd all felt, I wondered whether, in provoking those awkward feelings, the old lady had actually captured something of the heart of the first Christmas. The story of the birth of the Messiah is full of embarrassments.

There is the embarrassment of the young girl who was pregnant. The Bible said that God told Joseph the news in a dream. When one Sunday school teacher asked his class why they thought God used a dream to tell Joseph that Mary was pregnant, a little boy said, 'Miss, I think it was because God thought it best he was lying down when he got the news.' Her pregnancy was a great humiliation for Joseph, so much so that he was minded to call off the wedding.

And there is the embarrassment of being treated as a nobody. In their moment of great need, Mary and Joseph found there was 'no room' for them. In many ways it's a modern story – a story that will be repeated somewhere today. A young man who'd dreamed that it would be so different will say, 'I wanted better for you, but this is all there is.' And a young woman will be almost beyond caring *where* it happens, as long as her baby is finally born.

And what about that embarrassing episode of having shepherds come visiting – people considered so low and unreliable they weren't even allowed to give testimony in a court of law? The events of Jesus' birth were a series of embarrassments one after the other.

[167]

But God wasn't embarrassed. God was proud. So proud that he asked angels to sing in celebration.

I attended a church Christmas dinner for homeless people once. The event was not without its discomforting moments. A woman arrived drunk and insisted on waltzing with one of the church leaders, and one man ate the whole meal with his coat, hat and gloves on. Some of us might have found it embarrassing, but I am sure that Jesus wouldn't. And that's why, although the organisers expected 100 people, they did what they do every year; they laid places for 101 – an extra place for the unseen guest.

During that first Christmas, Mary learnt that it isn't an embarrassment when doing God's will brings you shame in the eyes of others. Perhaps the shepherds began to realise that God doesn't go along with society's view of who is worth knowing or not. And even though Joseph never got to experience the hospitality of the Bethlehem Hilton, he learnt that the God of the universe was watching over him and Mary. And there's no embarrassment in that.

No, the problem with the Christmas story was not that it was embarrassing for those involved; it was that there were some who were not at all embarrassed – those who were so sophisticated (religious leaders, government officials, royalty) that they missed it all.

The Bible tells us not to be ashamed of the gospel, and at the heart of the gospel is that first Christmas. When the old lady started to sing in the hospital ward that night, I think a few angels might have been joining in as well. It would be just like God to arrange a small choir.

I don't think he was embarrassed for a moment.

45

Who Am I?

DIANNE AND I have two children, both of whom are grown up with children of their own. Katie was our first and she was a very compliant child. It was Katie who lured me into the foolish belief that we were brilliant parents. Lloyd, our son, was sent to humble us. That little boy used to wake every day with the same prayer on his tiny lips: 'Dear God, help me drive my mother crazy today.' Every day God answered his prayer. And I mean *every* day.

Lloyd drove *me* crazy as well. In fact, when he was fourteen and I was at my wits' end with him, I did a deal with God. I said that if I could just live long enough to see Lloyd with a child of his own who gave him back just a little of what he'd dished out to me, then God could take me. I would die a happy man. (Perhaps that's why somebody said, 'The reason that grandchildren and grandparents get along so well is that they've got a common enemy.') I observe Lloyd now with his daughter, little Lily, aged two and a half. I watch, wide-eyed, as she stamps her little foot, shakes her head and wags a tiny finger. And I can't help thinking, 'Any day now . . . Swing low, sweet chariot!'

Grandparents are important, but the truth is that all older people have a vital role to play in the lives of the young. That's why the Bible places such emphasis on the stories and the values that the generations can pass on to each other. The long list of genealogies that we often skip past as we plough through our Bible-in-a-year readings are there because the importance of the family was understood in that culture. When children ask, 'Where did I come from?' they are often seeking much more than the biological details. Those lists of their ancestors helped children answer one of the deepest questions of human life: 'Who am I?'

It wasn't just a matter of knowing your family tree. Jewish culture recognised how vital it was to tell the old stories again and again. The Bible says, 'One generation commends your works to another' (Ps. 145:4). The book of Joshua talks of the Israelites being told to make a pile of stones taken from the River Jordan. And the reason for that? It was that the lessons and stories of faith would be passed on from the old to the young: 'In the future, when your children ask you, "What do these stones mean?" tell them the flow of the Jordan was cut off before the ark of the covenant of the LORD' (Joshua 4:6–7).

I love being around my young grandchildren. Perhaps it's because they seem to have an endless desire to hear my stories. Whereas my kids say, 'Oh Dad – not that old one', or, more sobering still, 'You told us that *yesterday*', the very young don't mind if you tell them the same story over and over again. The sadness is that although small children have an almost inexhaustible desire to listen to stories, in modern society most people seem to have little appetite or patience to make space to hear from those who are older.

I wonder whether we have slipped into that attitude in our churches? In most churches, the young and the elderly have very little interaction. What could we do to change that? How could we make opportunities for older people who have so much to give, to share with those who are young and have so much to learn?

And how can we make a better job of preserving the past in our families and churches? In African culture there is a saying, 'When an old person dies, a library burns down.' But the library shouldn't burn down. Perhaps we need to encourage parents, grandparents and family friends to take time to record the stories of their lives, their journeys of faith and life lessons learnt. I've spoken to people who were certain they had little to say when they began this task, but a few months later they had written journals bursting with stories or had recorded hours of memories. The past matters.

Anyway, mixing up the generations a little more is not just a one-way street; there are benefits for older people in being able to learn from the honesty of the very young. When my grandson Harry was being potty-trained, every time he managed the task successfully his mother said, 'Well done! You're a big boy now, Harry.' The other day, as she was cleaning up after a not too successful effort, Harry – seeming to realise that as you get older life gets more complicated and that what people demand of you increases every day – tapped her on the shoulder and said, 'Mummy, sometimes I don't want to be a big boy any more.'

I'm with you on that one, Harry.

46

Don't Look Back

I SIT WITH A church leader who has been challenged to try something new. The trouble is that few people know what he knows: the idea is *not* new. In fact, it is something he tried some years ago and it failed spectacularly.

As I listen to him list the reasons why this idea will never work, I realise that it will be almost impossible for him to make a rational decision about it because the events of years ago have such a strong hold on him. The past is a ghost in the cupboard that has now emerged to haunt him. It's a tattoo on his soul that says, 'Remember how this hurt you last time.' But that's not all. For my friend, the past may hold an even deeper terror: it may define his future.

The dreadful possibility is that what he dares to try

tomorrow will be restricted by the failures of yester-day. In some ways, though, it is right that the past is important to us. It is the memory of past childhood pain that keeps us, as adults, from touching the hot stove. We ignore the past at our peril. But sometimes the past does not just warn us – it paralyses us. Helen Mallicoat wrote a poem that urges us not to live like that.

I was regretting the past
And fearing the future . . .
Suddenly my Lord was speaking:
'My name is I am.'
He paused. I waited.
He continued.

'When you live in the past
With its mistakes and regrets,
It is hard. I am not there.
My name is not *I was*.

'When you live in the future
With its problems and fears,
It is hard. I am not there.
My name is not *I will be*.

'When you live in this moment,
It is not hard.
I am here.
My name is *I am*.'*

Whenever I ask an audience who their favourite disciple is, the winner is always the same: Peter. We vote for the failure – the one whose foolishness got him a rebuke on the mount of Transfiguration; the one who tried to walk on water and then sank; the one who boasted he loved Jesus so much, and then denied him until dawn.

Why does Peter command such affection from us? I think it's because he reminds us that our yesterdays need not define our tomorrows. His failures could have so imprisoned him that he never again felt the freedom to take a risk. But the past didn't have that hold on him. Perhaps he never forgot the words of the master, 'I have prayed for you, Simon, that your faith may not fail' (Luke 22:32).

Maybe I should remind my friend about Peter. And perhaps I could remind him, too, about another church leader who wanted to try something new. He was

* Helen Mallicoat, 'I Am', taken from *Holy Sweat*, by Tim Hansel (Word Books, 1987), p. 136.

approached by a nervous member of the congregation who said, 'But Pastor, what if it doesn't work?'

'No problem,' said the pastor. 'If it doesn't work, we'll just go back to doing what wasn't working before.'

47

Pride

ONE LIST OF them is over one and a half thousand years old, Morgan Freeman starred in a film about them, and there are a set of *Star Trek* novels based on them. They are the Seven Deadly Sins: lust, pride, gluttony, envy, sloth, anger and greed.

But which is the worst? Now to those who believe what I was taught in Sunday school – that all sins are equal in the sight of God (which, when I put glue between the pages of Mr Pendleton's copy of *Sacred Songs and Solos* put me on a par with mass murderers) – they are all as bad as each other. But are they?

Down the ages, it is pride that has been singled out as the most dangerous deadly sin. I wonder why. Perhaps it's because it's the easiest sin in the list to commit while having no knowledge of doing so. When it comes to lust, we know when we are leering at someone with less than pure thoughts. As for sloth, most of can recognise when we are bone idle and keep throwing sickies. And by the fourth tub of Ben & Jerry's, the gluttony button is normally flashing furiously. But how can we tell if we are proud? The Bible says that pride blinds us.

Of course, there's an even older list than the traditional Seven Deadly Sins one. It's in Proverbs chapter six and contains some pretty horrible wrongs – 'hands that shed innocent blood' (v.17) and 'feet that are quick to rush into evil' (v.18) being just two of them. But even in such frightful company, it is 'haughty eyes' (v.17) – a proud look – that takes the number one spot.

It's not easy to tell if we are proud, because pride blinds us. To the church at Laodicea the risen Christ said, 'You say, "I am rich; I have acquired wealth and do not need a thing." But you do not realise that you are wretched, pitiful, poor, blind and naked' (Revelation 3:17).

Being blind when you don't know it is a very dangerous thing. That's why the Bible says, 'Pride goes before destruction, a haughty spirit before a fall' (Proverbs 16:18). Pride whispers in our ear that God has a special set of rules just for us. We can be in the middle of an affair but up to our eyes in Christian ministry, so we still kid ourselves that we are right with God. The prophet

Obadiah said that when we are proud we say to ourselves, 'Who can bring me down to the ground?' Unfortunately for us, God says that he can: 'Though you soar like the eagle and make your nest among the stars, from there I will bring you down' (Obadiah 1:3–4).

I wonder if you or I could be guilty of the sin that caused the fall of Satan and that has, since then, destroyed countless leaders, ministries, marriages, friendships and even nations.

- Do we *really* listen when others are speaking to us – or are we itching to share our 'important' thoughts?
- Do we enjoy being 'noticed' in whatever position we may hold? Jesus said the religious leaders loved being recognised and called 'Master'.
- Do we pray? In other words, do we feel the need of God?
- Do we have time for people whom others perceive as nobodies?
- Do we sometimes catch ourselves thinking that God is fortunate to have somebody as gifted as us on his team – forgetting that he said, 'for every animal of the forest is mine, and the cattle on a thousand hills . . . If I were hungry I would not tell you' (Psalm 50:10–12).

- Do we have *close* friends? Somebody said, 'If you want acquaintances, tell them your successes. But if you want friends, tell them your fears.'
- Do we enjoy the successes of others?
- Does somebody else's pride really bother us? If so, ours may well be terminal.
- Do we willingly allow others to take the praise? Ronald Reagan used to have a plaque on his desk that read: 'There is no limit to what a man can do if he doesn't mind who gets the credit.'

Two humble ducks and a proud frog lived together in the pond. But one day the pond dried up. This was no problem to the ducks for they could fly, but it was serious for the frog. Then the ducks had an idea. 'We'll hold a stick in our bills, you stand between us and cling on to it with your mouth, and we'll fly us to a new pond.' As they soared away, high in the sky, the farmer saw them and yelled, 'What a clever idea! Who thought of it?' The proud frog couldn't resist. He shouted down, 'I did!'

Oh dear.

48

The Strugglers' Group

I WAS AT AN event held to launch Dianne's book, *You, Me and Coffee*. The place was packed and as the lights went down I settled back to listen to Di speak about what had inspired her to write it. I had no idea what was about to hit me: she began talking about something that occurred almost forty years ago and suddenly that old, anxious feeling stirred again in the pit of my stomach.

She said:

It was a beautiful autumn day, the sun was streaming through the bedroom curtains, and in so many ways life was perfect. I had a little girl aged three, a new baby boy, and I was lying next to my husband who loved me. The only problem was that I had just whispered to Rob, 'I don't think I can cope any more. Will you take Katie to nursery today?'

And so it began. Not something that would be over by the end of that day, that week, or even that year, but a journey into illness that defined our lives for a long time. Postnatal depression was part of it, and it seemed that Di's immune system was incredibly low. At least for the time being, the vibrant, funny, energetic woman I'd been married to for ten years was gone.

In her book, Dianne talks about 'tracing the rainbow through the rain'. This isn't about saying 'We're glad we went through it' or about applying a theological plaster to hide the wound. Rather, it is an acknowledgement that understanding and lessons were learnt during this time that changed the way we would live the rest of our lives.

One lesson was about the incredible power of weakness. A couple of years into her illness, Dianne said, 'Can we start a home group for people like us who feel broken, lost or just plain tired? We won't give them easy answers, but we'll share some of our own experiences, listen to theirs, and ask God's help for us all.'

And so, on a rainy Wednesday night, the Strugglers' Group was born. Over the coming months, all kinds of people flocked to it. I opened the door to a GP one evening and was so surprised to see him that I didn't even invite him in. He stood on the doorstep and simply said, 'I've come for the Strugglers' Group.' The variety in the ages, occupations and life experiences of the people who came was incredible. Those who were sure of their faith sat next to those who were quite sure they had no faith at all.

I remember saying to a very cynical social worker who had made it clear she had no belief in God, 'Gill, Di and I are struggling a bit as you know. I'm sorry you haven't got a better example of Christians.'

She said, 'You're fine.'

One night after everyone had left, the phone next to my bed rang. It was Gill. She said, '*He* has met me. As I drove home, I felt his presence in the car and an incredible sense of forgiveness. My heart is physically hurting. Will it be like this tomorrow?'

I said, 'I really don't know. It's never happened to me!'

So many of those who came to the Strugglers' Group, including Gill, are serving God today. During those evenings we learnt that most people's pressing need is to know that it's not just them. More than anything, what they want to know is that they are not alone – that you, too, have cried, doubted and messed up sometimes. It is this knowledge that helps silence the voices whispering to them that they alone have failed – as a husband/wife/ parent/friend/follower of Jesus. And even more than that, it can help open their hearts to the love of God.

It is for good reason that the Bible says, 'For when I am weak, then I am strong' (2 Corinthians 12:10).

49

For Better, for Worse

I AM WAITING FOR the wedding to start. The bride is five minutes late; her mother is already crying; the best man has been checking for the past ten minutes that he still has the ring; and the groom, although sweating profusely, is trying to look cool, as if he does this most days of the week. Suddenly the music starts and we are asked to stand.

I don't recall exactly how many weddings I've been to, but I can't remember one bride who didn't look amazing, or a single groom who did not, at least, look better than he'd ever looked before. We sing a hymn: 'Love divine, all loves excelling. Joy of heaven to earth come down'. Women turn and whisper to their husbands, 'This was one of our wedding hymns.' The men smile and nod – it seems the safest thing to do.

But then come the vows and it strikes me that these promises dare to invade this idyllic day with warnings of more difficult times. He says, 'I will love you if we are rich'; the vow whispers, 'But what if you are poor?'

She promises, 'I will love you for better . . . and for worse.'

He says, 'I will love you if you are well and . . . in sickness too.'

Will those vows ever be called in? Yes, they will – but the couple do not know that now. And then something from the Bible is read: 'Love is patient, love is kind . . . it is not self-seeking . . . It always protects, always trusts, always hopes, always perseveres . . .' (1 Corinthians 13:4–7). Yes, love is all those things. But the young couple do not know that yet either. On this most perfect of days, they cannot know yet that love is not just a feeling, but a daily commitment to love in action – to love sometimes not just with the heart but with the *will*.

But David knows it. He has been married to Beth for almost thirty years, the last ten of them watching her die slowly with a terrible wasting disease. He has lifted her, washed her and fed her. He has kissed her and held her all through those long years of sickness. It was not what he expected when he made his vows years ago. Yes, David has feelings of love for his wife, but his love is deeper than the emotion. It is a sacrificial love that decides to go on loving when at times it seems too great a burden. It is a love that, in some ways, lays down its life for another.

I remember speaking with a man who was leaving his wife and two young children for somebody younger who he said would better fulfil his needs. I asked, 'Why are you leaving your wife?'

He said, 'I don't feel in love any more.'

I treated him with dignity and with care, knowing full well the frailty of my own heart. But even as he was speaking, in the back of my mind there was an image of a man carefully feeding his wife and gently wiping the spilt food from her lips.

50

The Cross and the Chain

WHAT IS THE great search of our hearts as human beings? I have no doubt it is the endeavour to prove we are worth loving. And for many of us, this compulsion is all-consuming. Life screams at us that if we want to be loved we need to be clever, beautiful, sexy, wealthy. But life must have no idea how cruel it is to say such things. Does it not know that already our hearts are doubting that we are worthy of love? Our worthlessness wraps itself around us like a chain. It seems we cannot be free of it. We are imprisoned.

And then we come to Christ. The message of the great Lover's love pierces our very being. Suddenly our chains are cut off. We have never known such liberty. We run from the prison and scream into a blue sky, 'I am free – and I am loved.'

But for some of us the freedom is short-lived. It is a dark winter's night and we have already locked the door. We are surprised by the knock. We slide back the bolt tentatively and slowly to allow the darkness into the light of our home. A man stands there. He offers no name – simply hands us a set of chains and says, 'These are yours. You must put them on now.'

They are heavy; even weightier than the ones we left on the prison floor. We ask, 'But what are these chains? My chains are gone.'

The man smiles. 'Do you remember what you thought when you first heard the good news of the gospel – the news that God loved you?'

'Yes,' we say. 'It was almost too good to believe.'

'Well, in a way it was,' he says. 'You still have to prove that you are worth loving. You must prove it by your devotion, your work for the kingdom, your sincerity. Now, quickly, put them on; these are the chains of your freedom.'

As the years go by, the chains get tighter. They become not just the chains of our worthlessness but of our failure. Sometimes we work so hard for God, pray so hard *to* him, tell others so much about him, that we feel he must be satisfied. But he never is. Our work was for the wrong motives. Sometimes as we prayed, our minds wandered. Our witnessing was far too shallow.

Many of us die with the chains still wrapped tightly around our frame.

Lynne Hybels of Willow Creek Community Church described how one day she found herself crying out these words to God:

I can't do this anymore. I can't keep striving for your love. Maybe there is a God somewhere who doesn't drain the life out of people, but I don't know who that God is. You're the only God I know, and I can't carry the burden of *you* anymore.[*]

Who is the man who knocked at our door that night with chains? It may be that he is somebody from our church, or perhaps even the very enemy of our souls, but sometimes the man at the door has *our* face.

Our only hope is that there is another knock on the door. We open it in trepidation, clutching the chain the visitor passed on. But it is not he that has returned. No, another figure stands there – and he is holding broken chains.

'I have been knocking for a while,' he says.

We stutter, 'I did not hear you.'

'No matter now,' he says. 'Just give me your chains.'

[*] Lynne Hybels, *Nice Girls Don't Change the World* (Zondervan, 2006).

We protest, 'But the other man said . . .' And then we stop, for it is clear that this visitor has more power than any previous caller. He may say different things to each of us, but whatever he does say will cause chains to break.

When Lynne Hybels one day rediscovered the true God instead of the tyrant image she had grown up with, she felt him say to her:

I wasn't the one cracking the whip, the one telling you to work harder, the one who made you feel guilty when you relaxed. I was the one who saw you, who knew you, who believed in you . . . I was the one trying to love you.

We untwine our chains and give them to him. The second they touch his hands, they break and clatter as they fall to the ground. And suddenly we know in our hearts what we dared not truly believe in our heads: we are *loved*.

Free at last.

51

God's Will According to Cyril

WHEN I WAS a teenager, there was a boy called
Cyril in my church. Cyril was three years my
senior, but in his understanding of Christianity he may
as well as have been 300 years older. He went to hear
great preachers and took notes in a little book. And he
had a Bible with the words of Jesus in red and owned
something called a 'concordance', which he told me
allowed him to look up the word 'tabernacle' and immediately find every reference to that word in the whole of
Holy Scripture. It was obvious to me, even as a fourteen-
year-old novice, that somebody who had the capacity to
look up every reference to the tabernacle (whatever that
was) must be on very personal terms with God – a fact
of which Cyril assured me. Which is why I believed what
he told me about the Ecuadorian jungle.

We had just finished listening to a report from a missionary who was home on furlough. The second the man finished talking and switched off his slide projector, Cyril turned to me. 'Where is the last place on earth you would like to be a missionary?'

I had left my home town only once and that was for a week's holiday in Devon, so I didn't have a great deal of experience to go on when it came to the worst places in the world, but for some reason I blurted out, 'The jungles of Ecuador!'

Cyril replied in a flash, 'Then that's where God will send you!'

This was my introduction to understanding the will of God in my life, but through the years, as I progressed in my faith, I was able to grasp the finer details of Cyril's philosophy. Essentially, it worked like this: God will make it as difficult as possible for you to find out what he wants you to do, setting all kinds of tests, traps and false trails. Every little detail matters and you'd better not get anything wrong. In any case, when, eventually, you do discover what the Almighty wants, it is likely to be your worst nightmare. For this reason, it is not wise to pray that you will marry the girl in the youth club who looks like a supermodel. No – much safer to ask God to hitch you up with the draconian creature in the tweed suit.

It's easy to look back at our younger years and smile at our lack of sophistication, but I believe this view of the will of God is one that many of us still secretly hold. Such a belief condemns us to years of anguish over whether we have got it right or wrong in the past, and with regard to the future, it paralyses us with the fear of making an unwise decision.

Years ago, we employed someone in Care for the Family who had previously been homeless. He had just become a Christian and was looking for a job. We set him the task of entering data into a computer. After six weeks we discovered that he was an academic, and as we were looking for somebody to join our research team, we offered him the job. He was blown away. 'Wow, Rob! Just to get a job was great – but to be a researcher . . .!'

And then he hesitated, 'Can I pray about it and get back to you in a week?'

To be honest, I was a little put out, but what could I say? This was a new Christian who didn't have the spiritual wisdom about discovering the will of God that I had accumulated over many years! I smiled. 'Of course. Just let me know.'

Seven days later he was back in my office. 'Well, Rob, I prayed about whether I should be doing data entry or research.'

I was itching to know the result. 'What did God say?' I asked.

The young man smiled at me. 'He said, "Either's fine with me – you choose!"'

I was dumbstruck. It sounded so wonderful – so liberating. Almost as if God was his Father. Cyril would have had a fit.

52

Perspective

THE GIRL WHO ran up to me with a painting of her street was six years old. I took it from her as if I was handling a Monet. I said, 'It's amazing!' OK, so perhaps 'amazing' was a little over the top, but all the elements of the street were there: the houses all had doors and windows, the lamppost was just about where it stands in real life, and the cars looked like . . . well . . . cars. But there was one thing that was wrong – the thing that kept me, and perhaps you, from ever getting an A in art: perspective.

A lack of perspective doesn't just affect child paint-ers, and getting it wrong can have far greater conse-quences than a dropped mark or two in school. Some time ago, the pilot of a USAF jet pulled on the joystick to thrust her aircraft up and out of the clouds – and crashed into the ground. She was suffering from 'spatial disorientation'. For the past few minutes, she had been flying upside down; her perspective of reality had deserted her.

The concept of perspective is easy to grasp when we think of it in terms of a long line of houses stretching into the distance, and perhaps we can imagine losing our perspective in the cockpit of an aeroplane when the instruments let us down in bad weather. But, actually, it is perspective – or sometimes a very limited perspective – that often determines our actions and outcomes in life.

Consider this situation for a moment: a man is leaving an office party and a work colleague offers him a lift home. She stops her car 100 yards from his house, turns off the engine and says, 'Jack, I know that things aren't so good between you and Suzie at the moment. If ever I can help . . .' He's had a couple of glasses of wine, the aroma of her perfume fills the car, and now she moves closer to him. At that moment, his total perspective is confined to the tiny space that fills the inside of the Ford Mondeo and the prospect of the immediate pleasure of a brief kiss; a kiss that tells him he is still attractive to women – and still wanted.

Since that night years ago, Jack has replayed over and over in his mind what happened next. He has often wondered how such havoc could have been unleashed by something that was done so easily, but with the limited perspective of the moment he could not have known how it would all end. If only he'd somehow been able to see the text she'd send him an hour later that said how special their time together had been; if only he could have heard the phone call she made to his wife a week later after his rejection of her offer to meet again; and if only he could have foreseen the looks on his children's faces as he hugged them in the hallway of his home on the day he finally left, he would never have accepted the lift that changed his life for ever.

How can we get a longer and wider perspective? It's not easy. Perhaps we can do so by talking with friends and being honest with each other; perhaps by taking time to consider what we see happen in the lives of others. But let me suggest another source of help: the book of Proverbs. Proverbs tries to prevent us from having to learn lessons the hard way by telling us how our actions in various life situations will often turn out.

Describing the outcome in a similar scenario to the one I mentioned above, Proverbs puts it like this: 'he followed her . . . like a deer stepping into a noose . . . little knowing it would cost him his life' (Proverbs 7:22–23). The ancient book whispers to us, 'I will show you the next frame of the film. I will show you how, so often, it all ends. I will give you *perspective*.'

53

Look After These Little Ones

I REMEMBER WATCHING A film in which the mob put a rival into 'concrete boots' and hurled him into the sea. It reminded me of a passage from Matthew's Gospel: 'If anyone causes one of these little ones . . . to stumble, it would be better for them to have a large millstone hung round their neck and to be drowned in the depths of the sea' (Matthew 18:6). It was this kind of death that Jesus said was preferable to being alive and causing harm to a child.

Some scholars suggest that the harm Jesus talks about could be child abuse, and if they are right then it's not hard to understand Jesus' anger. And if we can't understand that anger, we should talk first not to children, but to adults whose lives are still blighted by the sense of utter helplessness they felt as children who were abused.

I think now of a businessman in his mid-forties who has just joined Alcoholics Anonymous for the third time to try to rid himself of his addiction. The great sadness is that even if he succeeds, he will still not be able to free himself from the memories he has tried to blank out with drink – memories of the visits to his childhood home of the wealthy uncle who came bringing gifts and tragedy.

When I was on a trip to Asia with Tearfund, we visited projects that sought to help and support children who had been abused, particularly in the sex trade. All the stories were heartbreaking, but one in particular stands out for me because the abuse suffered was not at the hands of some Western tourist but a man in the child's church. And the child's pain was compounded because for years nobody took her complaint seriously, not even her pastor.

Yet we should have some sympathy for church leaders who have to deal with these issues. One leader told me recently that a registered sex offender had asked to join his church on his release from prison. 'I had a whirlwind of emotions,' the leader said. 'I wanted to offer this man help in starting a new life, but I was terrified that he might harm a child in our care.' He agonised over the decision and finally told the man that he would be allowed to join the church provided that he agreed some boundaries. This included having someone shadow him each time he attended church – someone from a small group of mature people who would be with him at all times. And, of course, he would never be allowed involvement in activities where he would be with children – a protection for the children and the man himself.

But not all churches take the issue so seriously. David Pearson, the founder and former CEO of The Churches' Child Protection Advisory Service (now renamed Thirtyone:eight), commented, 'Too many churches are extraordinarily complacent when it comes to responding to children who might have been abused.' One leader of a small church was heard to say recently, 'We simply don't have that problem here.'

Perhaps that leader should speak to the child whose fear was not quite so readily brushed aside. Even after the man who had abused her had been made to leave her church, she was haunted by a single question: 'When I get to heaven will he be there?'

54

The Wisdom of a Postman

ARE INTELLIGENT PEOPLE wise? Not always. Intelligence and wisdom do not necessarily go together. Somebody said, 'Intelligence is your *how* power – your skill set; wisdom is your *why* power – your value system. Intelligence gives you a ladder; wisdom helps you decide which wall to lean it against.'

Some time ago, a friend gave me a great tip to get some more wisdom. He said, 'There are thirty-one chapters in the book of Proverbs. Read one a day for a month and then start again at the beginning.' Last week I read a verse I have come across many times before, but it struck me with fresh poignancy, 'The borrower is slave to the lender' (Proverbs 22:7). I think it caught my eye because I'd just read a report stating that households are going back to debt levels not seen since just before the financial crash of 2008.

My father was a postman. Was I more intelligent than him? Well, if exam passes are anything to go by, I beat him hands down. Was I wiser with money than him? No. He used to recite to me regularly that well-worn passage from *David Copperfield*: 'Annual income twenty pounds, annual expenditure nineteen nineteen and six, result happiness. Annual income twenty pounds, annual expenditure twenty pounds ought and six, result misery.'*

Some people don't need a clever talk on how to make ten meals out of two chicken legs – they simply need more income. But for most of us, that's not the issue: we spend about 10 per cent more than we have coming in, and until that changes we will forever be in debt. Wisdom understands that.

Another of my father's sayings was, 'Out of debt, out of danger.' Today we are taught to embrace debt as a friend and there is no doubt that it can be – perhaps a mortgage on a home – but it is often an enemy. Einstein called compound interest the eighth wonder of the world. Well, perhaps it is a wonder, but it's not a friend when it comes to debt. Martin Lewis, who founded the website MoneySavingExpert.com, gave a sobering example: 'If a 21-year-old borrows £3,000 on a credit

* Charles Dickens, *David Copperfield* (Bradbury & Evans, 1850).

card and makes the minimum repayments, they will be almost 50 before it clears.'*

My father liked to use cash. Not credit cards with all their simplicity, ease and security – *cash*. Some time ago in Care for the Family we ran a project called Cash for a Month. We challenged people to forgo using plastic for four weeks. Direct debits and standing orders for things like mortgage or rent payments would continue as normal, but for other spending we asked them to take out an amount of cash every Monday that would see them through the week. Some people divided the cash up and put it in various pots marked 'Food', 'Entertainment', 'Petrol', etc. Almost all who took on the challenge said they spent less. One couple said, 'We decided to go to the cinema one night, but we only had £4.80 in the entertainment pot so we stayed in.' And a woman told us, 'I was in Asda , tossing stuff into the trolley, when I suddenly thought, "Hang on, have I got enough cash on me to pay for this stuff?" I threw things in a lot more slowly after that!'

I remember coming downstairs very early one morning shortly after I got married. It was still dark and I put my head in my hands and started to cry. I whispered to

* https://www.moneysavingexpert.com/credit-cards/minimum-repayments-credit-card/ [accessed 16 July 2020].

myself, 'How on earth am I going to get out of all this debt?' If you'd looked at two men, the old postman and the rising young lawyer, and asked, 'Which one is in trouble financially?' you'd have got the answer wrong. But the ancient book of wisdom would have got it right.

Wisdom may not always get you through examinations, but it will help get you through . . . *life*.

55

Coming of Age

THE THEOLOGIAN HENRI Nouwen was very conscious of what he called 'clock-time' and often asked himself, 'Can I still double my years?' When he was thirty he said, 'I can easily live another thirty!', and when he was forty he pondered, 'Maybe I am only halfway!' Some years before he died, his question became, 'How am I going to use the few years left to me?' But then he reflected that an overemphasis on clock-time is based on the wrong belief that 'our chronology is all we have to live'. He realised that our life on earth is not simply about *chronos* – a Greek word for time that emphasises number: it is also about *kairos* – another Greek word for time that the Bible uses to describe 'opportunity'.*

* https://henrinouwen.org/meditation/god-loves-us-from-eternity-to-eternity/ [accessed 16 July 2020].

I think Henri Nouwen's later reflections are right. I am quite convinced that although the Bible urges us to 'number our days' (Psalm 90:12), this is more to do with realising that life is short – whatever age we are when we die – rather than encouraging us to obsess about how many years we have left. No, the eternal God is more concerned with *kairos* time and the opportunities that our remaining years offer us.

Today is my birthday and I have just opened a card that says on the front: 'If you didn't know how old you are, how old would you feel?' I can't get that question out of my mind; perhaps that's because although I know other people have reached the age that I am now, I am convinced that with me it's some kind of dreadful mistake.

I'm not sure how to explain it. It's as if the angel in heaven responsible for doling out the years of our lives in an orderly fashion got bored when I was forty-five and decided to press the 'fast-forward' button. Unfortunately, out of all the people on earth he could have chosen to experiment on, he chose *me*. I rocketed from midlife to bus-pass ownership at breakneck pace.

And so I stand in the hallway of my home, put my glasses on, gaze at the card and muse, 'If I didn't know how old I am, how old would I feel?'

My first choice is sixteen. Happy days! I played rhythm guitar in a rock band. We didn't have much time to practise – we were too busy deciding on the name for our group. We finally settled on The Blue Jets. We never made it big, but our drummer did. Dennis left us and joined a group that got three number one UK hits and ended up playing for the Bee Gees.

My second choice is twenty-five. This was a good time because I wasn't old enough to know how much I *didn't* know. When I was twenty-five, I could tell you why God allows suffering and how, on that final day, God will deal with those who have never heard of Jesus. And I didn't have one single question about hell.

Perhaps thirty years old? At that age, when our marriage was young and our children small, family traumas were what happened to other people. I believed when I was thirty that neither Dianne nor I would ever wake up one day and say, 'I don't think I love you any more.' And I was sure that our children would never cause us a moment of real worry. Or that I would ever be stupid enough to get us over our heads in debt.

Forty looks attractive. It was when I finished in the legal practice to begin a new charity, Care for the Family. What a blessing to leave behind all those whingeing clients who had no real appreciation of the great lawyer they had on their hands. What a relief to start a Christian ministry and say goodbye to all those letters of complaint. Actually, on reflection, perhaps forty wasn't the best age either!

Fifty wasn't so bad. By then I had enough letters of complaint to wallpaper my house and for some reason they didn't look as scary as they used to – some of them even seemed justified. At fifty, I had a better perspective on life and had begun not to take myself so seriously.

But the question asks not how old I'd like to be, but what age I really *feel*? I turn the card over in my hand, ponder the years that have gone, and suddenly, in my heart, I know the answer. I am ten. Sometimes I feel confident and at other times scared. Sometimes I feel like the team captain and at other moments worried that I might be the one they pick last. I remember that when I was a child I used to worry that one day my mother wouldn't come home from work and now I know she won't. And people tell me that time will heal, but it doesn't – and I still miss her.

But most of all I feel like a child because the older I get, the more I feel totally dependent on God. It's true that the Bible talks about moving on from childhood to adulthood, but there are elements of childhood that I am meant never to lose, and I find myself crying out time and time again, 'Father – help me!'

Anyway, it's not just about the serious stuff. In really boring board meetings and when the chairman's not looking, you might catch me trying to make the person opposite me laugh.

I know we're meant to grow up . . . just don't rush me.

Acknowledgements

It has been such a privilege to write for *Premier Christianity* in one form or another for almost thirty years. I am so grateful to Sam Hailes and all the other wonderful editors I have worked with over that time. I have loved it!

Thanks to Andy Lyon, Jessica Lacey and the whole team at Hodder & Stoughton.

Thank you to my agent Eddie Bell of the Bell Lomax Moreton Agency.

Thanks to Kate Hancock and the team at Care for the Family. And to my wife Dianne; we lived so many of these articles together.

And finally, a massive thank you to Sheron Rice; you made it a better book – again.